Getting Married

Elizabeth Martyn

 CONSUMERS' ASSOCIATION

Which? Books are commissioned by
Consumers' Association and published by
Which? Ltd, 2 Marylebone Road, London NW1 4DF
Email address: books@which.net

Distributed by The Penguin Group:
Penguin Books Ltd, 80 Strand, London WC2R 0RL

First edition April 1999
Third edition July 2004

Copyright © 1999, 2002, 2004 Which? Ltd

British Library Cataloguing in Publication Data
A catalogue record for *Getting Married* is available from the British Library

ISBN 0 85202 991 8

For a full list of Which? books, please call 0800 252100, access our website at www.which.net, or write to Which? Books, Freepost, PO Box 44, Hertford SG14 1SH.

Cover and text design by Kysen Creative Consultants
Cover photograph by Maria Taglienti-Molinari/(Brand X Pictures) getty images
Editorial and production: Joanna Bregosz, Lynn Bresler, Nithya Rae

Typeset by Saxon Graphics Ltd, Derby
Printed and bound in Great Britain by Creative Print and Design (Wales) Ltd, Ebbw Vale

Contents

* An asterisk next to the name of an organisation in the text indicates that their details can be found in this section

Introduction

There's never been a better time to be organising a wedding. The whole industry has shaken itself up, and offers couples everything they could possibly imagine to create the wedding of their dreams. The Internet is an invaluable source of ideas, advice, inspiration, products and services.

Although the traditional white wedding in church still happens, it is on the wane. The proportion of civil marriages continues to rise, as it has done since the advent of approved licensed premises in 1995. This has made it possible to have a civil wedding that looks like a traditional white wedding in a huge range of settings beyond the local register office. Within the next couple of years the choice of place and time for both civil and religious weddings will become even wider, as reforms to wedding law come into force.

More and more couples marry abroad, and there is also a rise in the popularity of following a simple civil marriage with an alternative ceremony, which, although it has no legal standing, allows couples unlimited choice in the way they organise the occasion. Another trend is towards themed weddings, which go far beyond merely matching the flowers to the napkins, and involve planning the whole day around a theme, with venue, clothes, music and entertainment chosen to fit.

One reason why the face of marriage is changing is that on average people are not marrying until they are in their early thirties. These couples are independent, 70 per cent of them are already living together, and many have children who will play an important part in the day. Another factor is the number of second marriages. In 2002, four marriages out of every ten were remarriages for either one or both partners. Many of these couples have children from previous relationships to consider when it comes to planning their wedding. For all these reasons, many couples are looking to break with tradition, or at least to include some very personal elements in their wedding day, and create a ceremony and reception that are not run-of-the-mill, but very much their own creation. The couple's parents may have a very significant role in the organisation, and may foot a proportion of the bill, but they seldom do all the planning, as was the case in the past. Instead, the majority of couples organise, and pay for, their own weddings

One thing remains certain, however. Whether your wedding takes place in a hotel or a village church, a register office or a medieval castle, and whether you have 20 guests or 200, the occasion calls for careful planning. This book will help you to organise every last detail, and contains checklists and budget sheets which you can enlarge and use to monitor the arrangements and, most importantly, the budget. There is comprehensive information on every aspect of organising and personalising all types of ceremony and reception. The book also has advice on how to finance the wedding and how to make financial plans for the future. There are guidelines on wedding etiquette, and suggestions on how to bend or break the rules to fit your own circumstances. Above all, your wedding should be the day that *you* want, a day to remember for the rest of your lives. The business of cakes and dresses, cars and champagne pales into insignificance beside the real purpose of your wedding day, which is simply to make a public declaration of your mutual love and commitment.

Chapter 1

Getting engaged

For most people, becoming engaged to be married is a big step, not to be taken lightly. Whether you will be leaving your parents' home for the first time, have been living with your partner for years or are marrying for the second time, the decision to tie the knot is a momentous and exciting one. Although some couples dispense with any trappings of formal engagement, for most the time leading up to the wedding is one when they can enjoy making plans together.

Announcing the news

If you have children, they should be the first to know of your plans. After them, courtesy and tradition demand that you should tell the bride's parents, who will, after all, probably make a financial contribution to the wedding. Ideally, you should visit them together unless long distance means that a phone call is the only option. The man does not need to ask his fiancée's father for permission to marry her, although he might like to do so as a mark of respect and consideration for his future father-in-law, if it seems appropriate. Whether you ask permission or not, the bride's parents will welcome a chance to talk to you together about your plans for the future. Next, you should tell the groom's parents – again, in person if you can. After that other family members and friends can be notified. If you create your own wedding website (see pages 68–9) you can include details of your engagement.

Formal announcements

An announcement in the local paper or one of the nationals is a good way to spread the news. Check the paper's website, or ring the

'Births, Deaths and Marriages' column a week or so before you want the announcement to appear. You may be able to send copy by email.

Traditionally, the bride's parents announce their daughter's engagement, but couples who live independently of their parents, or who are marrying for the second time, might prefer to make the announcement themselves. Standard formal wording is as follows, but you will see other versions in the engagements columns in any newspaper.

Mr G R Evans and Miss L A Thompson
The engagement is announced between Graham Ralph, younger son of Mr and Mrs Anthony Evans of Guildford, Surrey, and Lesley Anne, only daughter of Mr and Mrs Malcolm Thompson of Reigate, Surrey.

In the version below, the groom's father is deceased and his mother has not remarried:
... between Graham Ralph, younger son of the late Mr Anthony Evans and Mrs Martha Evans of Guildford, Surrey ...

In this version, the groom's mother has remarried:
... between Graham Ralph, younger son of the late Mr Anthony Evans and Mrs Martha Morgan of London ...

If the bride's parents have divorced but neither has remarried, it would say:
... Lesley Anne, only daughter of Mr Malcolm Thompson of Reigate, Surrey and Mrs Susan Thompson of Winchester, Hampshire.

If the bride's parents have divorced and the mother has remarried, it would read:
... Lesley Anne, only daughter of Mr Malcolm Thompson of Reigate, Surrey and Mrs James Wallace of Winchester, Hampshire.

An informal announcement (usually in a local newspaper), made by the couple themselves, could be:
Mr G R Evans and Miss L A Thompson
Graham Evans and Lesley Thompson are delighted to announce their engagement.

Engagement party

You might like to have a party or gathering of some kind to mark your engagement and to introduce your fiancé(e) to friends and family who have not yet met him or her. This could take any form you like, from a drinks party or a sit-down dinner to a night out at a club. You could also use it as an opportunity to announce your engagement, if you can arrange the party before the news gets around. Whether you have a party or not, you will probably receive some engagement gifts, and should send a thank-you letter for these immediately from you both.

Introducing the parents

If the two sets of parents have not already met, then you should do your best to set up a meeting as soon as possible. You could arrange a lunch, dinner, or even a weekend stay if they live far apart. If you are planning a lavish wedding you will almost certainly be looking to both sets of parents for financial help, and this initial meeting would be a good time to start the all-important discussions about the wedding budget and who will pay for what (see page 34). However, if a meeting is impossible, then an exchange of letters between the two sets of parents would help to reduce any feeling that they are meeting as strangers on the wedding day.

Choosing engagement and wedding rings

An engagement ring, though not compulsory, is a lasting token that many couples enjoy choosing together. The range of styles is enormous so decide on a price limit, then browse round a few jewellers' windows to get an idea of what is on offer.

The classic engagement ring, with a diamond solitaire, is still the most popular style. The cut of the diamond (the number of facets) is important because the more facets the diamond has, the more it will sparkle. The 'carat' value, which in diamonds is a measure of weight, is reflected in the price, and the heavier and larger the diamond, the more expensive it will be. The very finest, and most expensive, diamonds are completely clear and flawless, but stones

11

with tiny flaws, visible only under magnification, can still be very beautiful and are cheaper. However, you do not need to restrict your choice to diamonds. The other precious stones – emeralds, rubies and sapphires – as well as a wide range of semi-precious stones, from agates and aquamarines to topaz and turquoise, are all beautiful and can either be set alone or in combination with diamonds.

Gold and other metals

When used in rings, gold, which in its pure form is too soft for daily wear, is alloyed with other metals. The 'carat' value of gold refers to its purity, so 18-carat gold is purer and darker in colour than 9-carat, but also less durable. Most wedding rings are made of 18-carat gold, but people who do heavy work may choose a tougher 9-carat ring. White gold, which is alloyed with silver, is another popular choice, and rings are also available in matt gold and rose gold as well as in combinations of colours.

Platinum, a beautiful silver-coloured and very hard-wearing metal, is also available and is more expensive than gold. Silver is cheaper than either gold or platinum but is less hard wearing. It tarnishes and will start to wear thin over the years and show signs of knocks and scratches.

What type of design?

The choice is wide, and you may well be able to find exactly what you want in a high-street jeweller's, particularly if you are looking for a traditional setting. If you do not see anything you like, you can have a ring made for you. You can either choose one of the jeweller's existing designs or have one made up to your own specification, using the stones and metals you particularly want, although this is a more expensive option. Antique rings can be very attractive and often have dainty settings and unusual combinations of stones. Go to a reputable antique dealer and get the ring checked by a valuer before buying it. One other option is to wear a family engagement ring. If it is too large or small, a jeweller can adjust it to fit you.

Almost all women, and 80 per cent of men, wear a wedding ring, and the traditional plain gold band, which comes in a variety of widths, colours and cuts, remains highly popular. For something different, you could look at engagement and wedding ring sets, where the two rings are designed to match, and may interlock. A plain band studded with diamonds or other gems can double as engagement and wedding ring; or you could choose a Russian wedding ring, with three interlinked gold bands of different colours, a claddagh (clasped hands) ring or a signet ring.

Rings can be engraved inside with your wedding date, initials or any short wording you choose. This usually takes four to six weeks.

Tips for choosing the perfect rings

- Remember, you will wear the rings for the rest of your life. A high-fashion ring might seem like fun now but could look sadly dated in 20 years' time.
- Try on lots of different rings to find the weight and style that suit you. Something that looks great in the jeweller's window may look quite wrong on your finger.
- Choose engagement and wedding rings that are made of the same metal and carat, otherwise they may wear each other down as they rub together.
- Make sure the rings fit well. If you buy on a hot or cold day your finger measurement may not be a true gauge of fit.
- Take time to choose and keep an open mind. The right rings will give you daily pleasure, so it is worth taking care when you choose.

Q *Can a man wear an engagement ring?*

A Yes, he can wear an engagement ring, an engagement/ wedding ring set to match the woman's, a signet ring or any other sort you choose. Otherwise, you could give him a wedding ring that can be worn on a different finger until the wedding day. Some men do not like wearing rings, in which case he could have another item that he can wear all the time, such as a neck chain or watch.

Caring for your rings

Engagement rings with intricate settings can quickly pick up grime and grease, and stones lose their sparkle with daily wear. When buying the ring, check with the jeweller which is the best way to clean it, as some stones are particularly delicate and should not be immersed in cleaning liquids. Always be gentle when cleaning and have the settings checked occasionally. Some jewellers will steam-clean your ring while you wait.

Many people like to wear their wedding ring all the time, but engagement rings should be taken off when doing rough chores to avoid damaging them or scratching delicate surfaces in the home. Rings with 'rub-over' settings, where the gems are set flush with the band rather than standing proud, can take more everyday wear and tear than some other designs.

Remember to add your rings to your household contents insurance (see Chapter 21). A costly ring could be worth more than the single-item limit, which in many policies is £1,000, and should be itemised separately on the policy and covered at all times, not just when in your home. When you buy your ring, ask for a valuation certificate and keep it safely, together with a photograph of the ring(s) if possible, as it will be needed if you ever need to make a claim. Valuations need to be redone every three to five years, otherwise insurance companies may not accept them.

Alternatives to engagement rings

If you do not want to wear an engagement ring, you could choose another piece of jewellery, such as a necklace, locket or bracelet, instead, or buy some art or other memento for your home.

Preparing for marriage

No one marrying today can be unaware that in Britain more than two marriages out of every five end in divorce. Second marriages fail at an even higher rate than first ones.

Marriage preparation courses run by Relate★ are available in some parts of the country, and their book, *Before You Say 'I Do'* (page 231) also has useful information to help people gain a deeper understanding of what it takes to make a marriage flourish. Relate suggest that couples planning to marry think about the major events that might happen during their marriage, such as parenthood, loss of employment or serious illness, and consider how these might impact on their relationship. Good communication is vital. Being unable to talk to each other openly is at the root of most marital problems. Arguments that are not well resolved are another problem area, and the book and courses explain techniques for dealing with disagreements. Among the major causes of rows identified by Relate are money (number one on the list), attitudes to child-raising, arguments over the frequency of sex, and difficulties in agreeing over who does what around the house.

Prenuptial agreements

Prenuptial agreements – contracts signed by couples before they marry – once the province of the rich and famous, have become widely used in Europe and the United States, but are not legally binding in England and Wales. The prime function of a prenuptial agreement is to itemise the division of assets in the event of a divorce, but it can also include expectations in regard to sharing the responsibilities of housework, childcare and so on.

Although prenuptial agreements are not recognised in law, there are signs that English courts are becoming prepared to take them more seriously, and there is a gradual increase in the number of couples wanting to make such an agreement. Reasons for having a prenuptial deal could include:

- to ensure the outcome of a divorce in the future, thus also saving costs and unpleasant wrangling
- to protect family property
- for the very wealthy, to protect assets from claims made by a marriage partner, especially if the marriage is short-lived
- to protect assets built up independently, particularly for couples who both have considerable resources and are not financially dependent on each other
- for couples marrying for a second time, to protect the needs of children from a previous marriage
- couples who are of different nationalities might make an agreement to arbitrate over their financial matters in another country.

At the moment there are no government plans to legalise prenuptial agreements, but it is possible that more judges will start to honour them, provided that they have been fairly entered into, with separate legal advice given to both parties, and full disclosure of both sides' assets, subject to the interests of any children of the marriage.

For a small fee you can download a prenuptial agreement from a legal website such as Desktop Lawyer*, and this is the kind of document that would be required if the law were called upon to enforce your contract in the future. Before you embark on any discussions, be aware that prenuptial agreements of any type can arouse powerful emotions, and couples have been known to call off the marriage because the negotiations involved in making arrangements over the future division of assets caused too much bad feeling between them.

Every couple will have to decide for themselves whether some kind of prenuptial agreement has any place in their relationship. Whether or not they want to draw up a formal document, all couples would be well advised to discuss the way they see their future lives together taking shape. Talking over questions such as whether you both want children, how you plan to manage spending and saving, who will take responsibility for what in the home and for the care of any children you have, can help to clarify differences of attitude and might avoid problems later on.

While many people are happy to marry in the expectation of a lifelong tie, where problems will be resolved as and when they occur, others find that discussion (or even making a written agreement) helps to focus their thoughts and highlight exactly what is involved when entering into a marriage.

If the engagement is broken off

However upset and embarrassed you may be about breaking off an engagement, remember that it is easier to unpick a wedding than it is to unravel a marriage. It is very common to have occasional doubts as the wedding approaches; almost everyone suffers from last-minute nerves or the urge to escape from the pressure. But if your fears are more serious and persist even during the enjoyable parts of the preparations, it is far better to talk your concerns over with your partner and halt the proceedings, even if only for a short time.

If you do decide to break off the engagement, you do not need to give any explanations. Relatives and friends can be informed quietly, and if you originally placed an announcement in the newspaper, a brief notice of cancellation is all that is needed, simply stating your names and the fact that the marriage will not now take place.

Traditionally, if the woman breaks off the engagement, she should return her ring to the man. If he breaks the engagement, then she may keep the ring, although she may prefer to return it. Any presents the couple have received should be returned to the givers.

Chapter 2

What kind of wedding?

One of the first decisions you need to make is whether you would like to have a civil or a religious ceremony. Couples with a religious background who want their church's sanction on their marriage will naturally choose a religious ceremony. However, there are many reasons why nearly two-thirds of couples choose a civil ceremony, and these are discussed below. You may have to take the thoughts and feelings of your families into consideration but ultimately you should choose the type of ceremony you both want.

Once you have made your choice, you can go on to consider where the wedding will take place. Changes in the law scheduled for 2005/6 will open up a wider range of venues for both civil and religious weddings, but currently, for a civil wedding in England, Wales and Scotland you have a choice of the register office, or a wide selection of other approved premises. For a religious marriage, your choice will probably be limited to either of your parish churches, although in Scotland a religious marriage can be held anywhere. The mood you want to create – formal or informal – and the number of guests you want, and can afford, to invite, will both influence the sort of place you choose.

Civil weddings

Nearly two-thirds of all weddings are civil ceremonies, that is those which take place in a register office or other authorised place. Although the wording used differs from that in a religious ceremony, a civil wedding can be just as solemn and meaningful as a religious one (see page 143 for full details of the civil service).

You might choose a civil wedding because you have no religious beliefs, and feel that marrying in church would be meaningless or hypocritical. Perhaps your beliefs differ to the extent that a religious wedding is impossible. If one or both partners are divorced, then arranging a church wedding may be difficult (see page 222 for details). Some people opt for a civil wedding because they want a quieter, less lavish wedding than is sometimes involved in religious proceedings, although this is not to say that civil weddings have to be low key.

Some religious ceremonies, for instance Hindu and Sikh, usually take place in premises that are not licensed for the solemnisation of marriages, and so the couple must by law have a civil ceremony as well. (See the Appendix for legal requirements.)

Register offices

Most civil weddings take place in register offices. To find out where your local register office is, look under Registration of Births, Deaths and Marriages in the phone book. You are not tied to your local office however, and may marry in any office in England or Wales, provided you live in either country. Some register offices are in beautiful buildings and are much more appealing than others. Many local authorities have smartened up their marriage rooms, and all are now committed to customer care and providing a high level of service. Your local authority may have a website with details of all register offices in your area, plus information about options for the ceremony.

You will probably be allowed to personalise your ceremony with readings or music, but check with the superintendent registrar beforehand. No religious content is allowed in any additions you make to the ceremony.

Approved licensed premises

A civil wedding can take place in a register office, or in an approved venue. Almost 4,000 venues are registered in England and Wales, and you can marry in a hotel, country inn, stately home or castle, or somewhere far more unusual, like the boardroom of a football club, a zoo, a museum, or high up in the London Eye. Some venues are only suitable for the actual ceremony, while in others you can have both ceremony and reception under one roof. Contact details of all licensed venues are available on the website of the General Register Office for England and Wales*. For more detailed information, look at one of the specialised publications or websites, see Wedding venues section in Contacts (page 234).

In 2002, new Scottish legislation made approved venues available there for the first time. Over 400 places were registered, including highly romantic settings in castles, on board a ship on Loch Ness, by the Callnish Stones, on Kenmore beach or in Jedburgh Castle jail. For more details, visit the website of the General Register Office for Scotland★. During the first year of the new law, 30 per cent of marriages in approved venues were between couples who had travelled to Scotland especially for their wedding, neither of them being resident there.

New legislation in force in Northern Ireland from 1 January 2004 means that marriages there are conducted by authorised officiants, and there are now no registered buildings, so that religious marriages can be conducted in any place that the religious bodies consider appropriate, while civil marriages can take place in register offices, or in other authorised places. For more details, visit the website of the General Register Office (Northern Ireland)★.

Restrictions on approved premises

More venues are becoming licensed all the time. To gain a licence the premises must meet the following criteria (but note that the law is more flexible in Scotland, see page 217):

- be open to the public (so your own home could not be licensed)
- be indoors (so weddings cannot take place in the open air)
- be fixed, so a ship, for instance, would have to be permanently moored. It is not possible to marry on board a ship while it is at sea
- be suitably solemn.

If the venue of your dreams does not meet these criteria – perhaps you want to marry beside a lake, in a ruined abbey, or simply in your own garden – then you could consider having a civil ceremony in a register office, followed by an 'alternative' ceremony at your chosen venue (see pages 26, 150 and 232).

Advantages of a wedding at an approved venue

- While register offices are generally small, and can seldom accommodate more than a handful of guests, approved premises tend to be larger, and some can hold up to several hundred people, so all your family and friends can be present.

- The ceremony and reception can take place at the same venue, so there's no break in the proceedings while people travel from one to another.
- Approved premises offer more flexible hours than register offices, and you should be able to book them for a whole day on a Saturday, and even on a Sunday or Bank Holiday, although you would need to persuade the registrars to attend.
- Using an unusual venue can make your wedding feel very out-of-the-ordinary, and unique to you.
- The proceedings can be given a more traditional feel than is usually possible in a register office. For instance, the bride may be able to enter to music, and walk down an aisle to join the groom. She can wear a white wedding dress, which sometimes looks out of place in a register office, and have a retinue of attendants which the space available in most register offices would not allow.
- You may be able to personalise your ceremony to a greater extent at an approved venue than at a register office, by adding more readings, live music, and even your own words to the service (see page 120 for more details). Once again, however, no religious content is allowed.

Themed weddings

Your wedding could be themed to suit the setting. A castle or country house could provide the perfect backdrop for a medieval, 1930s or Jane Austen-style wedding. Other options are to pick a simpler theme, and let a particular colour combination or season run through the day; or go for a theme such as Oriental, Colonial or Western. Browse bridal magazines and websites* for plenty of inspiration.

Religious weddings

In the Anglican church you have the right to marry in your parish church as long as neither of you has a former marriage partner still living and one of you lives within the parish boundaries. See page 222 for details of the Church's view on remarriage after divorce. Most ministers will expect you to attend services and preparation sessions to ensure that you understand the religious significance of the marriage service.

In England and Wales a religious ceremony may be conducted only in a church. In Scotland, however, it is the celebrant who is licensed, not the premises, and a religious ceremony may take place anywhere – at your home, on a river bank, in a historical building – as long as the minister agrees that the surroundings are suitable.

A Roman Catholic priest will expect you to be confirmed and may insist on a lengthy period (usually six months) of notice of your intention to marry as it is regarded as essential for you to prepare properly for such a serious commitment. (See pages 216–228 for legal requirements.)

Interfaith marriages

Some religions do not allow marriage to members of different religions. If you suspect there may be a problem make enquiries immediately, since if no compromise can be found you may be forced to have a civil ceremony.

- There is no objection to marriage between people of different Christian denominations if you belong to the **Church of England**, **Church of Scotland**, **Church in Wales** or **Nonconformist (or Free Church)**, such as **Methodist, Baptist or United Reformed**. If one member of a couple is a devout member of another faith, such as Judaism or Islam, the minister would need to be assured that that person could accept as binding the Christian marriage vows.
- A **Roman Catholic** must acquire a special dispensation from his or her priest in order to marry a baptised Christian from another church. A priest's dispensation is also needed if the marriage is to take place in a non-Catholic church. If a Roman Catholic wishes to marry a non-baptised Christian, or someone who has no faith, then a bishop's dispensation will be needed; your priest will know how to obtain this. The couple may be required to take a course of instruction on marriage and agree to do everything in their power to bring up their children in the Roman Catholic faith. The Association of Interchurch Families★ offer advice and help to couples of different denominations, usually where one partner is Catholic.

- In the **Jewish faith**, if either the bride or groom is not Jewish, he or she must convert before getting married. This could take two years or more, depending on whether the conversion takes place under the Orthodox, Reform or Liberal/Progressive authority. Conversion is complicated and demanding, involving instruction and an examination. The Council of Christians and Jews★ can offer advice to Christian/Jewish couples.
- **Quakers** require that a non-member who wants to marry a Quaker meet with at least two members of the Religious Society of Friends★, so that they can assess whether the person has sufficient understanding of the religious nature of the society for the marriage to be allowed.

Getting married abroad

Tying the knot in an exotic foreign location is becoming increasingly popular, with about 30,000 couples a year marrying abroad. Many people marry abroad because they want a quiet ceremony without the stress that accompanies a wedding in the UK. Also, if the ceremony and the honeymoon are in the same place, the cost is much less than the average UK wedding. There is a wide choice of destinations, and many major tour operators have dedicated wedding brochures, websites and phone lines (see page 235). Although it is possible to organise a wedding abroad yourself, most people use a tour organiser, who can offer a complete package. You can stay on at your wedding resort for your honeymoon or choose a two-centre package.

Exotic wedding venues

For a beach wedding, your choice could include: the Caribbean, Kenya, Mexico, Sri Lanka, the Seychelles, Mauritius, Hawaii and Thailand. In the USA you could get married in a chapel of love in Las Vegas – with an Elvis look-alike singing during the ceremony – or have a fantasy wedding in Disneyland, with Mickey Mouse as a guest. The truly adventurous might like an underwater wedding at Key Largo or marriage in a helicopter 1,000 feet above Orlando. Other options include a slope-side wedding in a ski resort, a ceremony in a game reserve in Africa or a marriage on the Equator.

The legal requirements vary from country to country with regard to minimum residency required, documents needed and so on. See page 227 for preliminary guidance on this, and check carefully with the tour operator, who will be able to give you a detailed checklist of what is needed. Some countries will not marry people of certain denominations or those who have been divorced, so check carefully before making any bookings. A marriage performed abroad in accordance with local law is valid in the UK as long as you would both have been legally entitled to marry in the UK. Check on the availability of a marriage certificate, as you may have to register your marriage in the UK in order to get a duplicate certificate. Your travel company can advise on this.

Limitations of getting married abroad

Although wedding packages are very popular, they can be basic. The standard package usually offers all the paperwork, a simple ceremony, a bottle of sparkling wine, a posy of flowers and a few photographs. If you want something more lavish, choose a company that offers a good range of extras, such as special transport, floral decorations, extra champagne, a video, more photographs, and a celebration dinner.

- If all you want is a simple ceremony with no extras, and you would have taken a foreign honeymoon anyway, getting married abroad can be an inexpensive choice, with the basic ceremony package ranging from £200 to £700, excluding the cost of the holiday.
- In popular resorts there may be several weddings each day, and you may have to queue for a licence. Tour operators can advise on less busy destinations.
- A beach ceremony can be very simple and brief; this is fine if that is what you want and you know what to expect.
- Although you might be longing for a quiet wedding with none of the hassle of guest lists and seating plans, your family and friends may feel left out. Some companies will organise a special deal for guests who want to travel with you and will even arrange to put them up at a different hotel so that you have some privacy. Alternatively, you could organise a blessing or party when you return home.
- Photographs taken at a wedding abroad may not be of such a high standard as those you would get at home.

Marrying a foreigner

If one of you comes from a country other than the UK, you will have to take various steps when organising the wedding. These will depend on the country in which you plan to marry (check with the relevant consulate).

An Anglo-Japanese wedding

Mark and Yumiko met in Osaka while he was travelling round the world before going to university. After living together for 18 months they returned to England and later went back to Japan to get married.

Yumiko's parents did all the organisation for the wedding. First, the couple were driven to a Japanese register office for a civil ceremony, which would be recognised under UK law. After this they were taken to a specialist dresser, who arranged Yumiko's hair in a traditional style, applied white make-up to her face and helped both Yumiko and Mark to dress in traditional kimonos. They were then taken to a Shinto temple for the traditional ceremony conducted by a Shinto priest. This was in Japanese, but Yumiko's mother had arranged for a translator to be present so that the English guests could understand what was being said. The couple sat side by side in the centre, with eight members of Mark's family – who had flown to Japan for the occasion – on one side. As a sign of courtesy towards Mark's family, only eight members of Yumiko's family sat on the other side. The couple did not have to do or say anything during the ceremony.

After the ceremony the two families went back to a nearby hotel where the couple got changed into more comfortable clothes before sharing an elaborate meal with their guests.

In the United Kingdom

A foreigner will generally be asked to produce a passport as identification when applying to marry in the UK. He or she should take steps to ensure that a UK marriage will be valid in his or her country of origin; the consulate will be able to advise on this.

In a foreigner's country of origin

To be married in a foreign country under the law of that country, a UK subject may be required to give notice of the intended marriage in England, Wales, Scotland or Northern Ireland, if that is where he or she is resident, or to the marriage officer of the country in which he or she lives, and then apply for a certificate saying that no impediment to the marriage exists. It is important for the individual to check with the consulate that the marriage will be recognised in the UK. The rules on this vary widely from country to country, so check carefully.

Alternative ceremonies

Those who find a religious service inappropriate and the civil ceremony uninspiring might like to consider an alternative ceremony. These are not legally binding, so you would need to have a civil ceremony as well, but the alternative service could be the main part of the wedding, to which most guests are invited, and could take place in any setting you choose.

Among the possibilities are Pagan, Druid, New Age, Viking, Spiritualist and Humanist ceremonies, or you could create a ceremony that is entirely your own. Useful books and websites are listed on page 232. For more details of what form an alternative ceremony might take, see pages 150–152.

One couple wrote their own wedding promises

Jane and Michael had a very quiet register office wedding, followed by a reception for friends and relatives. They had worked out between themselves a list of ten 'wedding promises' and after the speeches they stood side by side and read these out alternately. The final promise was 'never to argue when tired'. A relative produced a decorative copy of the promises on her computer and had it framed as a wedding present for the couple; it now hangs in their kitchen and is a daily reminder of the promises they wrote and made together.

Recognising gay and lesbian relationships

UK law does not, unlike that of Denmark, the Netherlands, Norway, Sweden, France and Germany, recognise same-sex partnerships. At the time of writing (April 2004), the Civil Partnership Bill 2004 has just been published. The aim of this Bill is to allow same-sex couples to have a formal partnership that in nearly all respects carries the same rights and duties that a married couple enjoy. The Bill contains detailed regulations about the contracting of a civil partnership, and procedure if such a partnership breaks down. Adoption, inheritance, tax and social security legislation will be amended to give couples rights which approximate more closely to those of married couples.

Discussion and amendment of this Bill in Parliament has not yet begun, and a good deal of the detail may be altered by the time it becomes law. It will take some time to come into force, and parts of it may become law before others. For up-to-date information, look at the government website or that of Stonewall (see page 236).

Meanwhile, there are various ways in which same-sex couples can recognise and celebrate their relationship, although none of these has any legal significance. In 2001 the Greater London Authority* introduced the London Partnerships Register. Same-sex (and heterosexual) couples, where one partner is a London resident, can have their relationships officially recognised, and declare their commitment to each other by signing the register in a ceremony at City Hall in London.

The Lesbian and Gay Christian Movement* can provide details of ministers who are willing to conduct blessing ceremonies for lesbian and gay couples. The Unitarian and Free Christian Churches* have a tradition of supporting civil and religious liberty, and can put you in touch with a minister who could organise a service for you. Celebrations of commitment have been held by local meetings of The Religious Society of Friends* (Quakers), but in order to participate couples need to be involved in the local Quaker community and in sympathy with its religious principles. For a non-religious ceremony, the Pink Triangle Trust* can arrange an affirmation ceremony. Pink Weddings* can arrange a blessing, affirmation, registration or celebration.

Chapter 3

Second marriages

The number of second marriages is increasing, and more than 40 per cent of marriages are not the first for either one or both partners. In some ways it can be harder organising a second marriage – which may be the first marriage for one partner – because the traditional etiquette doesn't 'fit', and family and friends may have views on the kind of wedding you should have, which don't match your own. See page 234 for details of websites where you can find information and advice, and ask questions. Much of the information given in this book is, however, just as applicable to those planning a second wedding as to those planning a first. Couples marrying for a subsequent time are far more likely to choose a civil setting and may also have children from previous marriages to consider when planning the day. They are also more likely to dispense with, or alter, some of the traditional wedding trappings. Hints on how to do this are given here, while page 220 gives information on the legal requirements concerning second marriages.

Before the wedding

Among the first people to know of your plans to marry should be your children, if you have them, and any from previous marriages. It's very important for your future happiness to build the best possible relationship with each other's children, so don't take their reactions for granted, and be sensitive in the way you tell them. Find an opportunity when you can tell them together, and don't break the news while you're in public. Give children time to absorb the news, and a chance to talk things over with you. Be prepared for questions about how their future will change and answer them honestly. Even if your children have grown up and left home, you should tell them about your plans early on, and give them a chance to share their reactions with you.

Your parents should also be told about your wedding plans as soon as possible, although there is no need for the man to ask the woman's father for permission to marry her. Think about how you are going to finance the wedding, and whether you are hoping for a contribution from either set of parents, before you tell them the news.

Finally, there is the sometimes thorny question of telling ex-partners that you plan to remarry. It is better that you should be the one to do this, even if you have a poor relationship with your ex. Whatever the situation, be prepared for a whole range of reactions, some of them unexpected. The same applies to telling your former in-laws, if you are still in contact with them.

If you want to make a formal announcement in the press, it can be made by the bride's parents if you want to follow this tradition, or you can make the announcement yourselves. See page 10 for wordings. If the woman is known by her previous married name, as she may be if she has children from her former marriage, this can be used in announcements:

Mr P W Wilcott and Mrs S E Adams
Peter Wilcott and Serena Adams are delighted to announce their engagement.

Changing your surname
If a woman has children from a previous marriage who will be living with the newly married couple, she may wish to retain her previous married name or to change the children's surname to her new married name. This is a sensitive issue, which should be discussed with all parties involved, including the children and their father, if possible, before taking any action. Other options for changing/not changing your name, and details of who to inform of any change, are on page 63.

Considering the financial implications of remarriage
It is sensible to give careful consideration to your financial affairs before you remarry, especially bearing in mind the sad fact that second marriages are more likely to end in failure than first. A few couples decide to have a pre- or post-nuptial agreement (see page 15), which sets out what should happen to your mutual finances and property in the event of a separation. Even if this approach does not appeal, you should study the financial implications of remarriage,

especially if either or both of you have children from a previous relationship. It is especially important to make a will in this situation, as marriage invalidates previous wills. See Chapter 22 for more details on this, and other aspects of financial planning.

What kind of wedding?

The majority of people who are marrying for the second time choose a civil setting, and are more likely than those marrying for the first time to wed in approved licensed premises rather than a register office. Using approved premises provides the opportunity to have a celebratory occasion with many of the frills usually associated with religious ceremonies. Another possibility to make your wedding day extra special is to have a register office marriage, followed by an alternative ceremony in which you have the option of including a religious element. See Chapter 17 for more details on different types of civil and alternative ceremonies.

A civil ceremony can sometimes be followed by a church blessing (see below for more details).

The situation regarding remarriage in church has changed since 2002, and the Church of England has now agreed that in 'exceptional circumstances' a divorced person may be remarried in church during the lifetime of their former spouse. See page 222 for more information.

In Scotland divorcees may marry in church at the discretion of the minister, who will want to know something of the circumstances of the breakdown of any previous marriages before agreeing.

Church of England service of blessing for second marriages

A minister may be able to arrange a blessing service following a civil marriage ceremony. A service was published some time ago and is available from the Church House Bookshop★, in a booklet called *Services of Prayer and Dedication After Civil Marriage*. If this service is not available in a particular area, there may be a similar one which has been authorised for use and the minister would be able to give details.

Preparing for the wedding day

Whether or not you invite a former spouse to your wedding depends on the circumstances. If former partner/s do come along, you should introduce them to other people simply by saying, 'This is Mark', rather than 'This is my ex-husband Mark'. Children of a former marriage are usually invited, and other members of your ex-spouse's family could be included if you think it is appropriate.

Invitations can be sent traditionally, as from the bride's parents, or, more usually, from the bride and groom themselves. See pages 82 and 85 for wordings. Family and friends will want to give wedding gifts, even if you have been established in your home(s) for some years. See page 91 for ideas of what to ask for. What you wear depends on where you get married, and your own inclinations. There is nothing to stop the bride wearing a traditional white wedding dress, particularly if the wedding takes place in approved premises where more formal clothes won't look out of place. It is traditional not to wear a veil at a second wedding. For other suggestions of what to wear, see Chapter 11.

Some couples dispense with all the usual wedding formalities, and keep the proceedings very simple. If you prefer to follow tradition, you can have bridesmaids and pages, and a best man. The bride can be given away by her father; by another relative, male or female, or by a friend. Couples who have children from former marriages often like to give them a special role on the day. See page 76 for suggestions. If just one of you has children, it is still very important to include them. There are websites offering advice for situations where this feels awkward or difficult (see page 234).

The reception

Full information on organising a reception is given in Chapters 19 and 20. Etiquette can be very flexible, and you can organise things to suit the situation. Whether or not you have a traditional receiving line depends on how formal you want to be, and also on whether it is the couple or their parents who are hosting the wedding. For a sit-down meal you can follow the traditional seating plan or adapt it to suit your needs. You could include your children on the top table, or have a small top table, just for the bride and groom and any attendants, and distribute other close family members around other tables. Follow your feelings when you do the organising, and if necessary ask people where they would be most comfortable sitting to be sure of keeping everyone happy.

Speeches at second marriages

The speeches are usually less formal, and the bride's father does not have to make a speech, as he will probably not have given his daughter away. He may propose a toast to the bride and groom, or the toast may be proposed by another friend or relative. Traditionally this would be a man, but there is no reason why a woman could not make the speech if you prefer. It is best to make clear to anyone who will be giving a speech that references to previous marriages and well-meaning 'jokes' about the fact that this is a repeat ceremony are to be avoided. The groom responds to the toast with thanks on behalf of himself and his new wife.

Chapter 4

Your wedding budget

Getting married can involve major expenditure, with the average traditional white wedding costing between £14,000 and £15,000 (including the honeymoon). You don't have to spend this much, though. There are plenty of ways to cut costs, but the most important thing to do, before you buy anything, is to decide how much you can afford and plan your budget carefully. See Chapter 5 for more details on financing your wedding.

The preliminary budget

If you take the time to plan your budget carefully, you will almost certainly save money. Make a long list – or copy and use the one in this book – of every conceivable item that will be needed for your wedding day. Be it large or small, put it in your preliminary budget and write a figure against it. Phone round suppliers, browse the Internet, check out wedding magazines, trawl the shops, compare estimates (but remember, these are not binding), and get an idea of how much each item costs (we give a guideline in this book – see pages 37–47).

When you have a ballpark figure for each item, add it all up and include a contingency amount of 5 to 10 per cent of the total cost for unforeseen expenses. It is important to include this sum since it will almost certainly be needed and should not be viewed as an optional extra. For example, if your absolute top limit is £10,000, you should work to a budget of £9,000, allowing for a 10 per cent contingency of £1,000.

At this point, if the total is more than you can afford, you may have to rethink your plans and cut out some items to meet your limit. For example, you could have two bridesmaids instead of six, make your own stationery, opt for a paying bar at your reception, or invite fewer guests. Be realistic about cost, and don't succumb to the temptation to underestimate deliberately.

Who pays for what?

It's useful to work out early on who is going to pay for what. The traditional responsibilities are shown in the box below, but few families stick rigidly to these traditions. Most couples foot a sizeable proportion of the bill themselves, often with some help from parents. The bride's family is still likely to pay for more than the groom's family.

Traditional responsibility for payment

The bride's family pays for:
- engagement announcements (in the newspapers)
- invitations and all other wedding stationery
- the bride's clothing
- the bridesmaids' outfits (but often the bridesmaids, or their parents, will pay)
- flowers in the church and at the reception
- photographs/video
- transport to church/wedding venue and reception for the bridal party
- wedding cake
- the reception

The groom (or his family) pays for:
- engagement and wedding rings (bride pays for groom's ring)
- cost of licence or registrar's fee
- all church expenses
- transport to church/wedding venue for groom and best man
- bride's and bridesmaids' flowers, buttonholes
- gifts for attendants
- hotel for first night
- honeymoon

The final budget

Once you have agreed on the limit for expenditure on your wedding (and the cost of individual items), you can start placing firm orders.

- Wherever possible get **written quotations** – which are legally binding – and ask for them to be made out in as much detail as possible. If you change your mind about anything you have asked for, confirm in writing.
- Keep careful **records of all expenditure**. File away all bills, receipts and so on and do not throw anything away. Keep notes of any deposits paid, when the final balance is due and how much it is.
- Consider opening a **wedding bank account**, so that all cheques come from a single source.
- It is very **easy to overrun your budget**. Keep yours on a tight rein by being aware that any extras – and you will be offered dozens – will add to the cost, and a few relatively small amounts can add up to a sizeable total.
- Bear in mind **hidden costs**, such as lost earnings from taking time off to organise the wedding; or the cost of travelling to choose a venue if you are marrying some distance from where you live.
- Naturally, you will change your mind about things and discover **items that were not in your original budget**. Look at the impact on the overall budget before adding anything.

'The hotel tried to overcharge'

When Susanna and Andrew booked their reception, months before the wedding, they were told that payment in full was expected a few days before the event. When the final bill came, it included a charge of £450 for the use of the (big) room. Fortunately, during their original visit Susanna had taken a checklist and against 'separate room charge?' she had recorded 'no'. The new hotel manager was not happy (remember that staff can change between the booking and the actual occasion – another good reason for keeping detailed records) but was forced to accept the situation. However, it was a stressful and unpleasant incident, which the couple could have done without just a few days before their wedding.

Negotiating discounts

It is quite often possible to get a discount on items for your wedding. You could offer to pay the full amount at the time of ordering, in return for, say, 10 per cent off, but be aware that if the company runs into financial problems before delivering, your money could be at risk. The late autumn, winter and early spring are relatively quiet for many wedding suppliers, who may be more willing to consider giving a discount in order to secure your business at these times than in the busy summer months.

Q *If I have to cancel the wedding, where do I stand financially with suppliers?*

A In this situation you will be in breach of contract and will usually forfeit any deposit paid. You may also have to pay compensation to, say, a caterer for any financial loss suffered as a result of your breach of contract. This would normally amount to any profit element the firm loses on your deal. However, the caterer does have a responsibility to keep losses to a minimum. The more notice you can give of cancellation, the better the chance that suppliers' losses will be small. If you pull out at the last moment, they will be unlikely to get another booking, and your liability may be greater. (See Chapter 21 for information on insurance.)

VAT

VAT currently stands at 17.5 per cent, but suppliers with an annual turnover of less than £58,000 are not usually VAT-registered, and not all goods are subject to VAT. However, most items associated with weddings attract VAT, with a few exceptions.

- **children's clothing** A child is defined as being under the age of 14, and the zero-rated clothes are only those that fit a child of 13 years or less (height 158cm, chest 84cm, waist 71cm, hips 86cm and shoe size 1½). However, if you have outfits specially made for your child attendants and you provide the dressmaker with the material, you will have to pay VAT on the material. You will have to pay VAT on the dressmaker's time only if he or she is VAT-registered

- **wedding cakes** (if they are supplied independently of other catering)
- **food provided by the caterer that requires further preparation by the customer** (such as defrosting, cooking, reheating or arranging or serving on plates) is not subject to VAT.

Look at estimates or quotations you receive to see if VAT is included or ask the supplier if there is VAT to pay. If there is, that particular supplier is VAT-registered, and you may be able to make savings by looking for one who is not.

Budget breakdown

The table overleaf shows how the average total cost of £14,500 for a traditional white wedding is made up. The cost of some of these items could be up to 20 per cent higher if you are getting married in London.

In reality, many couples spend somewhere near the average for the majority of their costs, make savings where they can or where the item does not feature on their list of priorities, and spend more where something – the reception meal, say, or the honeymoon destination – is particularly important to them.

What is not included

These figures do not include the cost of any other celebration, such as an engagement party or stag and hen nights. Miscellaneous costs, such as cash spent on the day and so on, are not included.

What it costs: the hard facts

Below are more details on the amounts given in the table overleaf, plus some cost-cutting suggestions. Bear in mind that these figures are averages and that there is wide variation around the country.

Church/register office/approved premises fees

For a Church of England wedding, the fee for the publication of banns is £18, the marriage service costs £180 and the marriage certificate £3.50. Total church fees can mount up to about £300 or

Item	£
Church fees	300
Bride's wedding clothes	1,000
Bride's going-away outfit	300
Bride's beauty treatments	100
Attendants' outfits	500
Groom's wedding outfit	250
Engagement ring	900
Bride's wedding ring	270
Groom's wedding ring	200
Transport	500
Photographs	500
Video	550
Flowers	400
Reception	
Hire of venue	850
Catering/food	2,500
Drink	950
Cake	300
Entertainment	700
Wedding stationery	220
Insurance	60
First-night hotel	150
Honeymoon	3,000
Total	**14,500**

more, which includes the cost of the organist, church choir, bells and heating. Each parish sets its own rates for these extras.

For a civil service at a register office, the cheapest possible wedding is £97.50, which includes £30 per person for the superintendent registrar's certificates, a fee of £34 for the registrar's attendance on the day of the wedding, and £3.50 for a copy of your marriage

(text continues on page 44)

Budget checklist

Item	Estimated cost	Actual cost	Who pays?	Deposit	Paid	Balance £
Press announcements						
Engagement						
Wedding						
Engagement party						
Wedding venue fees						
Bride						
Dress						
Veil or hat						
Shoes						
Lingerie/tights/stockings						
Jewellery						
Going-away outfit						
Beauty treatments						
Make-up						
Hairdresser						

(continued overleaf)

Item	Estimated cost	Actual cost	Who pays?	Deposit	Paid	Balance £
Groom						
Wedding clothes						
Going-away outfit						
Barber						
Bridesmaids						
Adults' dresses						
Adults' headdresses						
Adults' shoes						
Children's dresses						
Children's headdresses						
Children's shoes						
Pages						
Outfits						
Shoes						
Ushers' outfits						

Best man's outfit						
Bride's father's outfit						
Rings						
Engagement ring						
Bride's wedding ring						
Groom's wedding ring						
Transport						
Bride and father to ceremony						
Bride's mother and attendants to ceremony						
Groom and best man to ceremony						
Bride and groom to reception						
Attendants and bride's parents to reception						
Bride and groom from reception						
Photographs						

(continued overleaf)

Item	Estimated cost	Actual cost	Who pays?	Deposit	Paid	Balance £
Video						
Flowers						
Bride's bouquet						
Bride's headdress						
Bridesmaids' bouquets						
Bridesmaids' headdresses						
Buttonholes and corsages						
Wedding venue decorations						
Car decorations						
Reception decorations						
Reception						
Hire of venue						
Other hire costs (staff, furniture, crockery etc.)						
Food						
Drink						
Crèche service						
Entertainment						

Service charge/tips						
Other						
Honeymoon						
First-night hotel						
Holiday						
Spending money						
Stationery						
Invitations						
Postage						
Order of service sheets						
Menus						
Place cards						
Other reception stationery						
Wedding insurance						
Hen and stag nights						
Any other costs						
Contingency of 5–10%						

(continued overleaf)

certificate, issued on the day of the wedding. For a wedding on approved premises, the superintendent registrar's certificates again cost £30 per person. In addition you will have to pay a fee set by the local authority for the superintendent registrar and registrar to attend the ceremony, and will also have to pay any charge made for the use of the premises.

Bride's clothes

The average cost of a traditional wedding dress with veil, headdress and shoes is £1,000. If you want to spend less than this, you may be able to hire a dress for about £300. Another option would be to make your own (which can be cheaper as long as the pattern doesn't require a large amount of expensive material) – see pages 96–101. A secondhand dress could cost under £100, or you could borrow one from a friend or relative, which will cost nothing at all.

The average amount a bride spends on a going-away outfit is £300, but you could wear a dress or suit you already have if you prefer.

Bride's beauty treatments, make-up, hair

A budget of about £100 would cover some new cosmetics, a manicure and a session with the hairdresser on the day. To economise, you could get friends to give you a manicure and do your hair.

Attendants' outfits

The average total cost is in the region of £500, but this clearly depends on the number of bridesmaids and pages. Having the outfits specially made can be costly. Good, less expensive outfits are widely available in high-street stores. Other options are to make them yourself or look for secondhand ones.

Groom's wedding clothes

Hiring full morning dress costs about £60 and buying a suit off the peg costs between £150 and £300. Remember to allow for shirt, tie and shoes. If you already own a suit you like, you could wear that rather than buying new.

Rings

The average spend on an engagement ring is £900, and £270 for the bride's wedding ring. The groom's wedding ring generally costs about £200. There is a very wide choice of less expensive rings available in any high-street jeweller. Antique rings are also available across the price range. A family ring if you have one could make a cheaper alternative.

Transport

Expect to pay £400-plus for cars (two cars for about three hours). To save money, you could use cars belonging to family or friends.

Photographs/video

Using a professional photographer for the day for a traditional white wedding will cost about £500. This cost could be considerably less if you are planning a simpler ceremony and can go for fewer shots. A professional video of the day, starting with the bride's departure from her house and ending after the speeches at the reception, will also cost about £500. A shorter video, ending after the ceremony, costs £300 or less. You can save money by asking friends and relatives to take photographs/video for you, as long as you are confident that they'll do a good job. Work out a list of important photographs and make one person responsible for taking them so that no vital moment or person is left out.

Flowers

On average, couples spend £300 to £400 on flowers for the day. Costs vary quite dramatically depending on where in the UK you live.

- A fairly simple, hand-tied bouquet costs £60-plus, while a wired shower style starts at about £100.
- Fresh flower headdresses cost from £35.
- Buttonholes are around £4 each (for a carnation), corsages £7.50 to £10.
- Floral arrangements for the church could cost from £100 and decorations for the reception range from £150 upwards.

Flowers do not need to cost this much. A skilled friend or relation could arrange the flowers for much less. If another couple is marrying on the same day you may be able to share the cost of flowers at the church, or you could use the flowers that are already in the church. If you pay for extra flowers in the church, check whether you can take some of them to the reception venue. Flowers in season and simple arrangements cost less than hothouse blooms lavishly displayed and can be just as effective.

The reception

The number of guests is the crucial factor here, with 100 being the average.

- The average cost of hiring a venue for this number is £850.
- Catering adds another £2,500 to the bill.
- Allow £950 for drinks.
- The wedding cake costs about £300.
- Entertainment: as a guide, a band playing for 3 hours costs from £500.
- A DJ playing recorded music for 3 hours would cost from £300.
- A string quartet playing background music for 3 hours would cost about £600.

Ways of cutting the cost include:

- holding the reception at home, or in a hall, which is cheaper than a hotel
- having a finger buffet instead of a sit-down meal
- offering sparkling wine rather than real champagne
- making the cake yourself, getting a friend to make it (this costs about half as much as having one professionally made) or buying one ready-made from a supermarket and having the icing done professionally
- having a short reception, which does not go on into the evening, saves on the cost of entertainment and refreshments
- having a paying bar instead of providing all the alcohol yourselves, or providing drinks for part of the evening, then having a paying bar.

Wedding stationery

The average total cost of stationery is over £200, including invitations, order of service sheets and reception items (menus, place setting cards). It is cheaper to buy invitations ready-printed from stationers and fill in your own details. There are many software packages you can use to make your own wedding stationery (see pages 67–8). Instead of service sheets you can use the church's service and hymn books.

Wedding insurance

Comprehensive cover costs between £50 and £300 (see Chapter 21, page 200). You could decide to take the risk and save the money, particularly if you are having a small, simple wedding.

First night and honeymoon

The average cost of a hotel for the first night is £150, but you can save money if you spend your first night at home or at a simple country inn or hotel. An increasing number of couples have a two-week honeymoon abroad, often at a long-haul destination, which costs on average £3,000. A shorter stay in the UK or Europe would be cheaper, or you could rent a cottage, but make sure it is comfortable and well heated.

A couple who made money on their reception

Debbie and Adam were on a very tight budget. After a family register office ceremony, they asked 50 guests to a lunchtime buffet followed by square dancing. Both wore clothes they already owned for the ceremony, while Debbie found a wedding dress in a charity shop for £35 so she could look the part at the reception. As they had been living together for a couple of years they did not want household gifts, so instead asked everyone to contribute food or drink for the reception. They ended up with plenty of food. One aunt provided a whole dressed salmon, the groom's father gave a case of champagne, and puddings and salads were plentiful. What they had not expected was that some guests would give gifts of money instead of, or as well as, food and drink. These more than covered the hire of the hall, band, photographer, glasses and crockery and other incidental expenses, and they finished with about £50 in hand.

Chapter 5

Financing your wedding

Getting married is not just a major personal pledge, it also represents an enormous financial commitment. While a no-frills register office do (excluding entertaining your guests afterwards) costs just under £100, the average cost of a traditional white wedding (including honeymoon) is about £14,500 – although many weddings end up costing well over £20,000.

Although you won't have to pay for the cost of your wedding all in one go, you will need to have money available to pay deposits for wedding services – such as the reception venue, catering, wedding dress and photographs – as soon as you book them. Before you start spending, however, it is essential to have a reasonable idea of the total cost by drawing up a detailed budget – see Chapter 4. This will give you an idea of how much money you have to pay up front and will also help you decide how you are going to finance your wedding. This can be with savings, by borrowing or by using a combination of the two.

Saving for wedding costs

The cheapest way to pay for your wedding is with savings you already have. However, if you have no savings – or the amount you have saved is not enough – meeting the cost out of savings may not be an option. How you choose to finance it will depend on how much spare cash you have, how far in advance you have begun planning and how much your wedding is going to cost. The table opposite shows the approximate amount you would need to save over different time periods to pay for a range of wedding costs.

Even if saving the full amount looks impossible, it would be worth saving as much as you can in the months leading up to the wedding. If you have not yet set a date, you could consider postponing it for a few months so – for example – you can at least save up enough to pay all the deposits.

How much you need to save

Time available to save	Monthly saving required if your wedding will cost:			
	£5,000	**£10,000**	**£15,000**	**£20,000**
6 months	£800	£1,700	£2,500	£3,300
12 months	£400	£800	£1,250	£1,700
18 months	£300	£600	£800	£1,100
24 months	£200	£400	£600	£800

Figures have been rounded to the nearest £100.

Two properties?

If both you and your partner each own property, it could be worth moving in together before the wedding and selling one of them. Not only could you use some of the cash raised from the sale to put towards your wedding but you could also save the monthly amount that was going towards the mortgage. If it's not a good time to sell, an alternative would be to let one of your properties out.

Paying for your wedding with a loan

If you do not have any savings – or you don't have enough to meet the whole cost – you could look at ways of reducing what you plan to spend on your wedding, or you could take out a loan. However, you should be aware that, because of the interest you have to pay on the loan, borrowing will push up the cost of your wedding quite considerably.

And before taking the loan route, consider how you will feel in a few years' time when you may still be paying for the wedding. Then think hard about the sorts of financial commitments you are likely to have in the future. For example, are you likely to have children? Will you want to move to a bigger home and so be paying a larger amount towards your mortgage?

If you think your financial commitments are likely to be onerous within several years, try to borrow as little as possible and try to repay the loan over as short a time as possible.

The main ways of borrowing are set out below but however you decide to borrow, the most important thing to consider is how much you can afford to repay each month. This is because the consequences of not repaying a loan can result in your being taken to court and getting a bad credit record. Working out how much you can afford to repay also tells you how quickly you can pay off the loan: the longer it takes, the higher the total cost of the loan because there's more interest to pay.

Paying for your honeymoon

It is a good idea to pay for your honeymoon with a credit card because of the extra protection you get from the Consumer Credit Act. If you have a problem with anything you pay for by credit card (between £100 and £30,000) and your supplier won't help, you can seek compensation from your credit-card issuer. For example, if your honeymoon is a disaster because your hotel was a building site and you cannot get redress from the tour operator, you can claim the money from your credit-card company. You are often charged a fee for paying for the whole of your holiday by credit card, so to avoid this you could pay the deposit for it (minimum of £100) by credit card and the rest with cash (if possible). If you do this you will still be covered by the Consumer Credit Act.

Which type of loan?

Given the sums involved, it is unlikely that an overdraft on your current account is going to be sufficient – and given that your bank can demand that you repay an overdraft at any time, it's not a very practical option either.

Credit cards
Unless you have a sufficiently high credit limit on your credit card, it is unlikely to be suitable for meeting the whole cost of your wedding.

However, using a credit card for part of the cost could be worth considering, but only if you have a card with a low interest rate (you can get details of low-rate cards by checking the personal finance pages of the weekend press or going to www.moneyfacts.co.uk). You could also take out a card specifically for wedding-related purchases, which could provide a convenient way of keeping an eye on your budget.

Personal loans

A popular way of borrowing to pay for a wedding is to take out a personal loan – these are available from banks, building societies and other lenders. The virtue of a personal loan is convenience coupled with certainty. Based on how much you can afford to repay each month, you decide how much you want to borrow and for how long. Repayments are then fixed for the duration of the loan so you know exactly how much you need to repay each month – see the table below for typical costs.

Typical cost of an unsecured personal loan

Size of loan	1 year	2 years	3 years	4 years	5 years
		Monthly cost of a loan repaid over:			
Without payment protection insurance					
£5,000	£440	£230	£160	£120	£100
£10,000	£870	£450	£320	£250	£200
£15,000	£1,300	£680	£470	£370	£310
£20,000	£1,740	£910	£630	£490	£410
With payment protection insurance					
£5,000	£470	£250	£180	£140	£120
£10,000	£930	£500	£350	£290	£240
£15,000	£1,400	£750	£530	£430	£360
£20,000	£1,860	£1,000	£700	£570	£480

Figures have been rounded to the nearest £10 and are correct at March 2004.

When comparing the cost of personal loans, always make sure that you are comparing like with like: a loan repaid over two years is always going to look more expensive (in monthly terms), than a loan repaid over three years.

Another thing to watch out for with a personal loan is the extra cost of loan payment protection insurance which many lenders try to sell alongside the loan. This kind of insurance – which aims to pay out if you're not earning because of ill-health or unemployment

– is usually quite restrictive and it can push up the price of borrowing quite considerably. However, it's easy not to notice this – a common ploy in personal loan literature is to make the repayments with insurance look far more attractive than those without it or to print the rates without insurance in tiny, hard-to-read type.

Tip

Don't automatically assume that your bank is the best place to get a loan. Rates vary tremendously and high-street banks rarely have the best deals. Other lenders – Internet banks especially – often offer much more competitive rates. You can get details by checking the personal finance pages in the national press.

Secured personal loans

Most personal loans are unsecured although you can get personal loans which are secured on your property. Secured personal loans tend to be cheaper than their unsecured counterpart but the risk is that if you fail to keep up repayments, you could lose your home.

Increasing your mortgage

In terms of the monthly cost, a reasonably cheap way of financing a lump sum is to increase your mortgage (another type of secured loan) – provided your lender will let you. Even using the typical rate of 5.75 per cent charged by most high-street lenders (in March 2004), borrowing £15,000 would add about £70 to your monthly outgoings. However, this option is expensive in terms of the total interest charged. And – as with secured personal loans – if you don't keep up your mortgage repayments, you risk losing your home.

A loan from your insurer

If you have an endowment policy (a type of insurance-based savings plan), you may be able to borrow money against the current value of the policy. Your insurer will be able to tell you whether this is a possibility, and also what your expected monthly repayments would be so that you can compare them with other forms of borrowing.

'I did babysitting jobs to help pay for my daughter's wedding'

Barbara and Graham's daughter and her fiancé had set their hearts on a large white wedding, with a reception for over 100 guests at an Elizabethan manor country hotel. The estimated cost was between £10,000 and £12,000. The couple was able to contribute £4,000, and Barbara and Graham agreed to pay the rest.

'We had about £3,000 in savings and decided to take out a bank loan for £5,000 over two years. The repayments worked out at about £250 a month. So the only problem was where to get the money to repay the loan. A colleague then told me that she had been babysitting for a number of families and that there was plenty of work in the area. This struck me as a good way to earn some of the money to repay the loan and I was able to charge £5 per hour.

'It wasn't long before I was babysitting regularly and earning up to £80 per week. In the weeks leading up to Christmas and at New Year I was working every evening and once or twice stayed the night so that the parents could stay out longer.

'I babysat for about 18 months and earned £4,500. After that I worked less often and eventually stopped altogether once I had earned all the money I needed.'

Chapter 6

Planning ahead

All weddings, large or small, call for careful planning. You will need to make lots of lists and keep a close check on what has been done and what remains to be done. Book your key venues and suppliers as early as you can – you can think about the details later. Do not feel that you have to take care of every last item yourself; delegate wherever you can. In this chapter is a detailed list of what you should be doing when.

Wedding organisers

If you just don't have the time to make all the arrangements yourself, and there is no one in the family who can take on the job, you could use a professional wedding organiser. This industry is growing fast, as couples realise that using an organiser can both ease the burden of endless decision-making, and save them time.

Experienced wedding organisers are excellent managers and negotiators, and are very knowledgeable about where to get the best deals on services and supplies. They may be able to negotiate discounts that individuals could not achieve. You can use a wedding organiser to take over as much or as little of the arrangements as you like. Part of their job is to discuss with you exactly what you want and to refer back to you before making any final arrangements, so that you remain in control.

What a wedding organiser can do

- Deal with the legalities of a civil wedding.
- Help you personalise your ceremony.
- Keep a tight grip on your outgoings. You agree a budget with the organiser at the outset, and he or she organises the wedding

within those constraints. The organiser must provide you with a breakdown of costs, check contracts and monitor deposits and when payments are due.

- Recommend services and suppliers, such as photographer, florist, entertainers, and, if you wish, make all the arrangements with them, including negotiating prices. The organiser may well be able to negotiate discounts.
- Send out invitations and monitor replies.
- Oversee and co-ordinate all arrangements, both before the wedding and on the day.
- You can also have a one-off session with an organiser, or ask them to deal with just one aspect of the day, such as finding a venue that fits your particular requirements.

To find a wedding organiser, ask around your friends and colleagues for word-of-mouth recommendations. (See page 234 for more information on how to find an organiser.) Some approved licensed premises have an 'in-house' wedding organiser, who can co-ordinate the arrangements. Overseas tour operators may also have specialist staff who can oversee a wedding that is taking place abroad.

Before you sign any contract with an organiser, read the small print and make sure you know exactly what the terms are. Some charge a flat fee, which could range from around £200 for a one-off consultation to £1,500 for doing all the organising. Others take 10–15 per cent of the total cost, which would work out far more expensive if you are having a large wedding. Before you book, follow up a couple of references from previous clients and get a detailed written quotation, outlining exactly what the organiser will and will not do.

Soon after your engagement

- Decide what type of wedding you are going to have: religious or civil, formal or informal.
- Draw up your preliminary budget (see Chapter 4).
- Decide who will pay for what.
- Work out how many guests you can afford/want to invite and draw up a guest list.
- Choose and book location for ceremony and reception. See setting the date and time, page 56.

- Start browsing the Internet (see Chapter 7 and page 266) and checking bridal magazines for ideas on flowers, dresses etc. Keep everything in a box file. Start a wedding notebook and carry it with you. Use it to jot down ideas and note names, numbers, estimates, dates and so on.
- Find out if you need to make any special arrangements regarding a wedding licence (see the Appendix), and if so start the necessary procedures.
- Approach best man, attendants and vital guests to make sure they keep the date free.
- Book any of the following you want to use:
  photographer
  video maker
  florist
  transport
  caterers
  toastmaster
  entertainment for the reception.
- Order the wedding cake.
- Book the honeymoon.
- Start making arrangements if the wedding is being held abroad.
- Shop for dresses and accessories for bride and bridesmaids and order if these are being specially made.
- Start working out the details of the reception.

Allow plenty of time to make all the arrangements, particularly if you are both working, or are not already living together and so have less opportunity to discuss things. If you are getting married away from where you live – in your parents' home town, for instance – you will need to schedule in several visits to the venue to organise all the local services such as transport, flowers and caterers. You will also need to spend time in the evenings and at weekends on organisation.

Setting the date and time

- For a formal wedding allow a bare minimum of three months for the organisation. Six is better, and a year is not too long if you want to marry at a popular venue on a Saturday. Some churches and reception venues are booked up for many months in advance, especially for summer weddings.

- Compare diaries early on to make sure you avoid other commitments and ensure all the key guests are free on the date you have chosen.
- Church weddings are not usually allowed on Sundays. Saturday is the most popular day, although there is nothing to stop you choosing a weekday if the minister agrees.
- By law, in England and Wales, a wedding must take place between 8am and 6pm, although Quaker and Jewish weddings are exceptions to this rule. In Scotland a religious wedding can take place at any time as long as the minister agrees.
- A civil wedding at a register office must take place during the hours when the office is open, usually Monday to Friday, 9am to 4pm and Saturday mornings from 9am until 1pm. Approved licensed premises are likely to be more flexible over timings, and can be booked for a whole day and evening, if the reception is taking place at the same venue. It may also be possible to get married on a Sunday or public holiday at approved licensed premises, as long as you can persuade the superintendent registrar and registrar to attend, and can organise the other suppliers and services you need.
- Some Christian ministers prefer not to conduct weddings during Lent (the period leading up to Easter). If you are permitted to marry at this time, you may not be allowed to decorate the church with flowers.
- If you, or guests, are keen on sport, try to avoid the dates of major fixtures such as the FA Cup Final, which takes place in May, or the Wimbledon Final in early July.
- Venues and suppliers may give you a reduction if you marry between November and February (but not at Christmas or New Year), or on a weekday. Flowers, however, are at their cheapest in spring.
- If you marry on a winter's afternoon, the light outdoors may not be very good for photographs. Winter weather may also be a limiting factor if guests have to travel far.

Four to six months to go

- Order the wedding invitations (printing takes two to four weeks). Some couples send out invitations at this stage, so that people can make sure their holiday arrangements or other commitments don't clash with the wedding date. For a big wedding, sending invitations early leaves you time to send out a second round if many people refuse.

- Draw up a wedding gift list (or organise one at a department store – see page 90).
- If making your own fruit cake, bake it now.
- Contact the minister to confirm dates of the banns and details of the wedding.
- Book bellringers.
- Decide on the form of service and hymns you want for a church wedding.
- Arrange to meet organist and choirmaster to discuss choice of music, and book organist and choir or soloist.
- Book hotel for wedding night.
- Decide what the men in the wedding party will wear and buy any clothes needed.
- Consider arranging wedding insurance (see Chapter 21).
- Set up your own website (see pages 68–9).

Two to three months to go

- Arrange a rehearsal for the ceremony.
- Check passports; apply for new or amended ones if necessary (see pages 64–5).
- Apply for any visas needed for your honeymoon.
- Send out invitations six to nine weeks before the wedding, if you have not already done so.
- Check off replies as they arrive.
- Book overnight accommodation for any guests who need it.
- Send gift list to those who request it.
- Make a list of the gifts (and who they are from) as they arrive and write thank-you letters immediately.
- Meet caterers to agree food and drink menus.
- Buy wedding ring(s).
- Buy wedding gifts for each other.
- Buy gifts for best man and attendants.
- Book groom's, best man's and ushers' morning suits if hiring (allow six weeks).

- Buy your wedding shoes and underwear before your first dress fitting so you can try on the whole ensemble together. Wear the shoes around the house so they are comfortable on the day.
- Have first wedding dress fitting.
- Shop for going-away outfit.
- Shop for honeymoon clothes.
- Take your headdress along to the hairdresser to discuss a suitable style and have a trial run if necessary. Make an appointment for the day.
- Have a session with a beautician and try out any different make-up well in advance of the day. Make an appointment for the day.
- Book any beauty treatments you want to have before the wedding.
- Have any vaccinations needed for the honeymoon. Some can make you feel unwell, so choose a time when you can rest if necessary.
- Visit family planning clinic if necessary (see overleaf).
- Decide on bouquets, buttonholes, corsages and floral arrangements needed for church and reception and order them.
- Order other stationery such as order of service sheets and items for the reception or design your own on a computer (see pages 67–8).

One month to go

- Check that any guests who have failed to reply did receive their invitations.
- Draw up a draft seating plan if you are having a sit-down meal.
- Confirm date of wedding rehearsal.
- Hear banns read in church.
- Arrange for photographer to visit venue with you to prepare a list of specific shots.
- Prepare a newspaper announcement.
- Gather information for speeches and write drafts.
- Book manicure for the day before.
- Check that everyone in the wedding party has organised the correct clothing.
- Final fitting for wedding dress. Leave this as late as possible, since many brides lose weight before the wedding.
- Advise bank etc. of change of address and name (see page 63).
- Arrange stag night and hen party for at least a week prior to the wedding.

Your period needn't spoil your day

If your periods are very regular, either naturally or because you take the combined pill, five minutes spent with your diary will reveal whether a period is due on or around your wedding day or honeymoon. If this is likely to cause you a problem, talk to your GP or family planning clinic at least a month before the wedding day for advice on how you can use the combined pill to alter the dates on which your period will arrive. If you are not taking the pill, or use the progestogen-only pill, you could consider taking the combined pill for the short term in order to benefit in this way, but should take medical advice beforehand, as the combined pill is not suitable for all women.

If you have never taken the pill before, you should visit the clinic two to three months before your wedding, so that you have time to get over any of the minor side-effects which women often experience when they start the pill.

Alternatively, a doctor or nurse can prescribe other hormonal tablets which delay the onset of a period, without having any contraceptive effect. If you are going to a long-haul destination for your honeymoon be aware of the effect that passing through different time zones will have on when you should take your pill. Again, see your GP or clinic in advance for advice. The fpa (formerly known as the Family Planning Association) Helpline* can give advice on these and other matters.

- If you feel stressed over the next few weeks, give yourself a day off from thinking about the wedding, or try some distractions such as a long walk, a massage or a comedy show.

Two weeks to go

- Finalise and practise speeches.
- Ice and decorate the cake if making it yourself.
- Order traveller's cheques or currency for honeymoon.
- Confirm all the arrangements: florist, photographer, video maker, cars, reception, cake, church details and honeymoon.
- Have stag night and hen party.

> **Tip**
>
> Leave it as late as possible to finalise your seating plan and allow for some flexibility. People may cancel or decide that they can come after all just days before the event.

One week to go

- Wrap gifts for attendants, best man and each other.
- (Groom) place correct fees for minister, organist, choir, bell-ringers and church heating in cash in marked envelopes and give to best man, together with keys for going-away car on the day.
- Time the journey to the church so you know exactly what time you will need to leave home.
- Pack honeymoon luggage and check travel details and tickets. You can finish packing the night before the wedding.
- You may be offered the chance to have a wedding rehearsal a week or so before the actual day. This is so that everyone in the wedding party knows exactly what to do and when on the day. It is attended by the bride and groom, best man, chief bridesmaid and bride's father. Other, younger attendants may be included if you wish.
- Arrange for someone to take care of bride's dress and accessories after the wedding (usually her mother). The best man should take charge of the groom's clothes and, if they are hired, return them.
- Review the seating plan and prepare place cards.
- Confirm final number of guests to caterer.
- Think through the logistics of the whole day: who is doing what, when and where. Doing this will help you identify any last-minute arrangements that are needed.

The day before

- If using your own car to go on honeymoon, check that it has petrol, oil and water and is in perfect running order.
- Pack going-away/honeymoon clothes and if possible have case(s) taken to reception venue.

- Give the best man and attendants their presents.
- (Bride) have manicure.
- Double-check all the arrangements.

On the day

In the hours before the ceremony:

Timings given are for a traditional church wedding. Timings for civil weddings are given on pages 147 and 149.

- the bride has her hair done, does her make-up and dresses
- flowers arrive at bride's home
- bridesmaids arrive and change
- chief bridesmaid or bride's mother helps bride arrange her veil
- best man and groom dress in their wedding clothes
- best man checks that he has the rings
- groom gives best man any cash or cheques he may need to pay for church facilities etc. plus any travel documents etc. for the honeymoon
- going-away clothes are taken to reception venue
- going-away/honeymoon luggage taken to reception venue
- groom's car left at reception venue if it is to be used to leave the reception
- best man collects buttonholes and order of service sheets to take to church.

Shortly before the ceremony:

- ushers arrive at church 45 minutes before ceremony begins
- photographer and video maker arrive at wedding venue
- organist arrives at church and begins to play quietly about half an hour before the ceremony is due to begin
- minister, choir and bellringers arrive about half an hour before the service begins
- guests begin to arrive at the church and are given order of service sheets by ushers, who also direct them to their places according to the plan (see page 159)
- best man and groom arrive at the church about 40 minutes before the ceremony begins and pose for photographs, then take their positions in the front pew on the right of the aisle. Best man may pay the minister now or after the service

- bridesmaids and bride's mother leave for church and pose for photographs on arrival, about 10 minutes before the ceremony
- bride's mother is escorted to her place in the front pew to the left of the aisle. She leaves a seat on her right for the bride's father
- bride and her father leave for church and are met in church porch by bridesmaids. They pose for photographs. Chief bridesmaid arranges bride's dress, train and veil. Ushers take their seats in church. The minister greets the bride at the church door and can then either precede her down the aisle or return to the chancel steps and wait for her there. The choir can either head the procession or be already seated in the choir stalls.

Changing your surname

Every woman who marries has to decide whether or not to change her surname. You are not legally obliged to do so. See page 29 if you have children from a previous marriage or relationship. The various options are:

- **Changing to husband's surname** This is easy and makes any joint ventures straightforward. To make the change, send a copy of your marriage certificate to the relevant organisations (banks and building societies will want to see the original), so that they can change their records.
- Another common choice is to **keep your unmarried name for work purposes**, using the title Miss or Ms as you prefer, and use your married name and the title Mrs elsewhere. Think this through before you make any changes, as confusion can easily set in if you are not consistent. If your job involves a lot of travel, tell your employer if you change your passport and bank details.
- You can **both keep your original names**, which is straightforward, but can cause confusion.
- You could use **both your surnames, hyphenated**. If both of you decide to adopt a new composite surname, you will need to change your names by deed poll. You can do this online, at the UK Deed Poll Service★.
- Your **husband could change his surname to your maiden name**. However, unlike women, men do not have a legal right

to change their name on marriage, so he would need to do this by deed poll through the UK Deed Poll Service★.

- If you do choose to change your surname/s you should inform:
  your employer
  Inland Revenue for tax and NI records★
  bank
  building society or other mortgage or savings providers
  insurance companies
  credit-card and store-card companies
  passport office (see below)
  pension providers
  DVLA★ (the Driver and Vehicle Licensing Agency) to change driver's licence and vehicle registration documents
  Premium Bonds Office★
  utility companies
  telephone company
  mobile telephone company
  local authority, for council tax and electoral register
  investment companies
  Internet provider (and change email address)
  any companies of which you are a shareholder
  motoring organisations
  any professional associations to which you belong
  any other clubs or societies
  GP
  dentist.

Travel documents for your honeymoon and changing your passport

- If you are going abroad on honeymoon and wish to **travel using your married name**, you can change your passport from three months before the wedding. You do this by surrendering your existing passport. You will then be issued with a new passport showing your new name, which will be valid for ten years and up to another nine months depending on the remaining validity on your passport. This costs £42. If your present passport has children included, they will not be re-included on your new passport. You cannot use the new passport until the date of your marriage.

- You will need to complete a standard application form and a copy of Form PD2, completed by the person who will be conducting the ceremony. You can download an application form (but not Form PD2) from the website of the UK Passport Service (UKPS)*.

- The UKPS has over 2,000 High Street Partners, mostly post offices and travel agents, throughout the UK. Application forms and Form PD2 are available from High Street Partners and, for a handling fee of £5, they will forward all the relevant paperwork, plus your payment for the passport, direct to the Passport Service.

- **Check that the name on your passport and visa is the same as the name on your travel documents**. You can travel using your unmarried name and change your passport on your return; or if the tickets are in your married name, take your marriage certificate with your existing passport. However, some countries will not grant a visa on post-dated or amended passports, nor on a passport in your unmarried name accompanied by a marriage certificate. Check with the relevant consulate in advance. If you do change your name on your passport, remember to inform your tour operator as some assume you will be travelling under your unmarried name. It is frustrating to go to the trouble of changing your passport only to find you have to take your marriage certificate after all because your tickets are in your unmarried name.

Chapter 7

Online resources

The Internet is a fantastic resource for anyone who is planning a wedding, and the scale of what you can do on the web is vast.

- Loads of resources are available online to help you plan, such as budget templates, seating plans, task lists, and even Wizards to help you decide what needs doing first.

- You can use the web to help you narrow your search for the right caterer, photographer, venue etc. Almost every business of this nature has a website that will give you a feel for what they can provide without your having to visit in person or phone them. In addition, their website design and photos give an excellent indication of the style of service or supplies you'll be buying.

- Building your own wedding website is a great way to get far-flung friends and relatives involved in your big day.

- Weddings are expensive and some of the biggest outlays are for items that may only be used once. With the web at your fingertips you can easily find suppliers of second-hand goods, or sell your goods after the wedding and recoup some of the cost.

- Using a digital camera at the wedding, or scanning your professional prints into a computer afterwards, means you'll be able to share photos of the fun and festivities with all your guests and those who couldn't make it without the expense of endless reprints.

- It's possible to plan the complete wedding from a distance, using the web to source venues, caterers, celebrants etc. Couples living abroad, or a long way from where they plan to marry, will find this a godsend.

Wedding websites

There is a vast number of websites dedicated to helping you organise your wedding. A small selection is included in Contacts★, but this can't begin to do justice to the huge range of sites on offer.

Having said that, the content and quality of websites varies widely. Look for the suffix *.co.uk*, or look for a UK contact address on the site, if you are looking for a supplier in Britain. Sites from the USA and elsewhere can be useful when you're looking for ideas, even if you don't want to buy products from far afield.

Among the types of site you can expect to find are the following.

- General information sites, offering planning advice, etiquette pointers, ideas for clothes and much, much more. Many have links to suppliers, and may also have chat rooms, where you can swap ideas with other couples. Some sites will also host your wedding website for you.
- Directory sites, listing suppliers or venues by type and area, with links and other contact details.
- Specialised sites, concentrating on just one aspect such as wedding dresses or flowers.
- Online gift registries are very useful for guests from overseas or out of town.
- Sites which help you to create your own website and offer downloadable software.
- Local register offices may have their own site with details of venues and ceremonies available.

As well as going to specialised wedding sites, you can use the web to search for poetry and readings, ideas for music, speeches, honeymoon destinations and so on.

Wedding software

Wedding software packages are available from retailers but you will also find a wide selection for downloading from the web, sometimes for free. Search 'wedding software' on *www.google.co.uk* for a selection. Many packages are made in the USA, and may need to be adapted for British use.

Wedding software packages provide the templates and decorative images need to produce invitations, orders of service, menus, place cards and so on. To get the best results, print on good-quality paper, at the highest specification available on your printer. Some stationers stock packs of ready-made blanks of invitations and menus which you can customise with your own information.

Some software packages are designed only to create stationery, while others also have a planning element. Features vary, but you might find:

- budget planner, to track spending
- wedding gift list
- guest list
- seating planner.

If you are already competent on your computer, you may not need specialised software at all. Most computers have a wide range of fonts and decorative effects already installed, as part of a word-processing or desk-top publishing package. With a scanner and some picture-editing software you can add photos or illustrations of your choice. You could also use a spreadsheet or Word-based macro to create guest lists and address labels.

Your own wedding website

Setting up your own website is an excellent way to spread information about your wedding. As well as the practical details of your wedding, you could use the site to ask people to submit funny stories to be incorporated into the speeches, run your own online gift registry or even set up an email distribution list for all your guests so they can discuss travel arrangements, gift ideas or just get to know each other prior to the occasion. Search 'wedding album' on *www.google.co.uk* to see how couples have organised their websites. Ideas of what to include on your site include:

- pictures of yourselves as children, engagement pictures, the story of how you met and how you got engaged
- date and time of the wedding
- directions to the wedding/reception venue, with downloadable maps for guests to print
- details of local B&Bs and hotels, for those who need overnight accommodation
- 'cast list' of all the principal participants

- guest list
- wedding gift list – guests can consult the list then contact the store separately
- chat room where guests can ask questions or make comments. You can set up your own chat room on Yahoo!
- after the wedding you can post pictures of the day itself.

Creating a website

Most general wedding portals will host your site and provide a template and webtools for you to build it with. This is a quick, easy and cheap alternative to setting one up yourself, and means you won't need your own software or have to find an ISP to host the site or register a domain name. Doing it yourself is a viable option only if you are very keen or already know exactly what you're doing.

Putting pictures on your wedding website

There are two points to remember when putting photos or video clips on to your website.

- Don't put too many on one page, as this will slow down the rate at which the page loads. Put one or two on to a page, and use web links to step through the pages.
- Don't post the full-resolution images that you get from the camera, as these will slow the site down dramatically. Instead, use your photo-editing software to reduce the size of the image file (aim for a file size of 50 Kb per image and no more than 100 Kb per page).

Webcams

You could set up a 'live' webcam for the wedding or reception which would transmit images on to your website as they happen. A fair amount of computer and Internet expertise is required to do this, and you will also need access to a telephone line, or better still a broadband cable connection, not something that many churches or register offices can provide.

The webcam is connected to the computer, which itself is permanently logged on to the Internet. You need to set up webcam video capture software and web page posting to your web space. Special software is available but this is still a daunting task unless you are experienced.

The results are likely to be disappointing. Conventional, inexpensive webcams are generally fixed-focus devices which would give a low-resolution, broad-view image of the venue, meaning that much detail would be lost, and viewers would not be able to recognise guests.

An alternative, although equally complex, solution is to use a conventional camcorder with zoom lens etc. which is connected to a video 'capture card' fitted to your computer – which then transfers images to the Internet. The quality would be a little better than with a webcam, although the images are likely to be very jerky.

Chapter 8

Principal players

Who you choose as best man and attendants can make a big difference to the smooth running of your wedding day. Whatever the size and style of your wedding, you are going to need help, both on the day and before it. Think carefully before you decide who to ask and offer the roles to people who will enjoy them and whom you can trust to do a good job.

The best man

The groom usually chooses a relative or close friend for this job. Traditionally, the best man is single, but nowadays it is quite in order to choose someone who is married. The job can also be done by a best woman, or be shared between several people. The best man needs to be confident, dependable, a good organiser and someone who can be relied upon to stay sober throughout the proceedings. As well as giving practical help before, during and after the wedding, the best man is there to give moral support to the bridegroom both before the event and on the day. His responsibilities are listed below.

Before the wedding day he:

- helps the groom to choose the ushers
- organises the stag party and makes sure that the groom gets home safely after it
- arranges the hire of clothes for the groom, the ushers and himself
- attends the wedding rehearsal
- confirms all arrangements by liaising with the bride's family.

On the wedding day he:

- arranges for the honeymoon luggage to be taken to the reception venue

- briefs the ushers before going to the ceremony
- organises the ushers at the venue
- ensures buttonholes and order of service sheets are at the venue
- organises parking arrangements at the venue
- pays any church expenses on behalf of the groom
- drives the groom to the venue, ensuring that they arrive about 40 minutes before the start of the ceremony
- takes care of the wedding ring(s) until they are needed during the ceremony
- signs the register as a witness (optional)
- accompanies the chief bridesmaid out of church
- assists the photographer in marshalling guests for photographs
- ensures that all guests have transport to the reception
- arranges his own transport to the reception
- possibly takes part in the receiving line
- generally looks after guests at the reception
- keeps an eye on the clock so that proceedings don't overrun
- keeps an eye on any wedding presents brought to the reception and ensures that they are taken away safely afterwards
- introduces the speeches and toasts, reads messages from those who could not attend, announces the cutting of the cake
- delivers his own speech
- ensures the couple have transport from the reception and, if necessary, organises a non-drinker to drive them to their destination
- ensures that honeymoon luggage is in the going-away vehicle.

After the wedding he:

- takes charge of the groom's clothes and returns any hired items promptly.

Q *I can't decide whether to ask my brother or my best friend to be best man. Can I have them both?*

A Yes, as long as you can decide between you who is going to do what. Perhaps one could perform the best man's role during the ceremony, and the other could take over at the reception.

Q *I have always been very close to my sister and would like her support at my wedding. Can I have a best woman?*

A Yes, of course; you can choose anyone you like to support you.

The ushers

The number of ushers you will need depends on how many guests you invite to the ceremony. A rough guide is three ushers per 100 guests. They help seat people in the church or at a large civil venue and hand out order of service sheets. Again, choose people whom you know to be reliable and able to deal with any problems that crop up on the day. The ushers have the following duties:

- arriving at the venue early
- ensuring that order of service sheets are in place for the use of the wedding party and minister or registrar
- giving buttonholes to the principal male guests
- standing at the door and distributing order of service sheets or hymn and prayer books
- directing guests to their places. The bride's mother and other principal guests should be personally escorted to their seats
- helping any guests with small children or those who are elderly or disabled
- may take on other tasks as needed.

The chief bridesmaid and bridal attendants

Chosen by the bride, the bridesmaids are traditionally unmarried female members of her family or close friends. However, bridesmaids and pages may also be members of the groom's family. A married attendant is known as a matron of honour. Your own children, if you have them, can be bridesmaids or pages.

The very young attendants are not expected to do anything on the day except look decorative and behave themselves. Do remember, however, that although tiny bridesmaids and pages can look enchanting, they cannot be relied upon to keep still and quiet during the ceremony, so choose them with care and limit the number of those under five years old. The chief bridesmaid processes up the aisle behind the bride, followed by the other attendants. If you are planning to have a flower girl, whose job it is to strew the bride's path with petals as she leaves, do check that the minister has no objections. The chief bridesmaid is usually expected to:

- help select the bridesmaids' outfits
- organise and attend the hen party
- possibly help the bride choose her wedding dress
- help the bride to dress on the day of the wedding
- be in charge of the younger attendants, making sure they have their posies etc. and know what to do in the venue
- ensure the younger attendants are well-behaved in the venue
- arrive at the venue before the bride and help arrange her dress and veil before the procession goes in
- help the bride to lift back her veil at the top of the aisle
- hold the bride's bouquet during the ceremony
- perhaps witness the signing of the register
- leave the venue with the best man
- at the reception help the best man make guests welcome
- keep a check on the younger attendants at the reception
- help the bride change out of her wedding dress before leaving. She may also take charge of the bride's wedding clothes if the bride's mother is not doing this.

If you have other adult bridesmaids, they could help the chief bridesmaid with some of these jobs.

The parents of the bride and groom

At a church wedding, the bride's father traditionally escorts her down the aisle. This may also be possible at a civil wedding at approved premises. The bride may be given away or not, as she chooses. The bride's father also makes a speech at the reception.

The bride's mother has no formal duties, and most of her work goes on behind the scenes, ensuring that everything runs smoothly. She may play a major role in the planning and organisation of the day. If the bride is getting married from her parents' home then her mother may help her to dress on the wedding day, and make sure the flowers have arrived on time and that the best man has taken the buttonholes and order of service sheets to the wedding venue.

At the reception, the bride's parents act as hosts, greeting guests and seeing that their needs are met. The groom's parents traditionally have much less involvement with the proceedings, although they may well contribute both financially and with any practical help that they are able to give. The two families should liaise on the guest list, and at the reception both sets of parents take part in the receiving line (if there is one), greeting guests as they arrive and making introductions where necessary.

What happens when the bride's or groom's parents are divorced?

Where neither partner of the divorced couple has remarried, then ideally they should set their differences aside and sit together in the wedding venue and at the reception and stand side by side in the receiving line. If animosity makes this difficult or impossible, then they should arrange unobtrusively to have the least possible contact during the day without making the rift too uncomfortably obvious to others.

Where divorced parents have remarried, the mother sits at the front with her husband, and the father and his wife sit behind. In the receiving line divorced parents should stand together, while new partners should simply mingle with the other guests.

Q *My father wants to give me away, and so does my stepfather. How can we resolve this?*

A In theory, you should choose which one you feel closest to, and the other should respect your decision, which should be relayed with great tact and sensitivity. If that seems too difficult, an unconventional solution would be to ask your mother to accompany you down the aisle.

Witnesses

You will need two witnesses to sign the register at a religious or a civil wedding. The witnesses do not have to be 18, but must be old enough to understand what being a witness means. Think about who you would like to act as witnesses before the ceremony, and ask them if they would be willing. Some couples each nominate one of their parents, but you could ask a close friend, or a child from a previous marriage. Make sure that the witnesses are seated so that they can easily come up to sign the register at the appropriate moment. At a civil wedding, the registrar may ask for the witnesses to sit at the front, near the couple, for the whole of the proceedings.

Attendants at a civil ceremony

It is not usual to have bridesmaids and pages at a register office wedding, although it is not unheard of. However, you can have a best man, who can produce the rings at the appropriate moment, and the bride can ask a close relative or friend to give her special support on the day. If you marry at alternative licensed premises then you will be freer to make the occasion more like a traditional wedding and have as many attendants as you like.

Involving your children in your wedding

Many couples have children of their own, or from previous marriages, to whom they would like to give a special role on the day. There are lots of ways in which you can do this. Young children can be bridesmaids or pages, while an older son or daughter could give the bride away, be in charge of producing the ring(s) at the appropriate moment, act as witness, sign the register or be an usher. You can seat children directly behind you during the ceremony if space permits, or in the front row of guests. Most couples choose not to invite the other parent of children from former marriages, and if this is the case, or for your own children, you will need to ask another family member or friend to keep an eye on them during the ceremony. Children may also like to take part in the ceremony, or reception, by singing, playing an instrument or reading a poem.

Gifts from the bride and groom to the best man and attendants

It is customary to give gifts to the best man and attendants as a way of expressing your appreciation and gratitude for their contribution to your wedding day. Jewellery is a popular choice, and you could give the best man and ushers cufflinks, a tie pin or a watch, and the chief bridesmaid a necklace, ring or earrings. It is a good idea to give the same item to each of any younger bridesmaids to prevent comparisons, perhaps choosing something they can wear on the day. Watches are often popular with children and are a good choice for page boys. Ornamental keepsakes, such as a photograph frame or engraved mug, might also be suitable. Alternatively, you could break with tradition and give cameras, computers, portable CD-players or any other gift you think would be welcomed.

Many couples give the two sets of parents a gift to thank them for everything they have done to help. If you want to stick with tradition, a decorative item for the home, perhaps engraved with details of the wedding, would be appropriate, but again the rules are there to be broken, so choose what you know would be most appreciated by the people concerned.

Chapter 9

Wedding guests

The task of deciding who to invite to your wedding will be a difficult one. If your parents are making a financial contribution to the day, they will almost certainly want to have a say in who should be on the list and may want to insist that you invite certain relatives and family friends. You, on the other hand, may want to ask all your friends and include only close family members. This task will require diplomacy, and you will have to work out a compromise that suits everyone.

Before you start writing your list you need to work out how many people you are able to invite. Your budget and the type of reception you would like will influence this, as will the size of the wedding venue. For example, most register offices cannot accommodate more than 30 guests, in which case you could invite only the closest relatives and friends to the ceremony and extend the numbers for the reception. On the other hand, if you'd like to invite 100 or more guests, bear in mind that, with such a large number, you will probably spend only a couple of minutes talking to each person on the day.

Having decided how many people to ask, make a preliminary list, starting with the people who should definitely be invited – your closest family and friends. Then write down the names of those who you will probably ask – more distant family members and friends. Finally, list those who you would like to ask if numbers allow, such as colleagues and acquaintances. Aim for equal numbers for bride and groom, although this might not be possible if one partner's family is much larger than the other's, for example. See page 31 for advice regarding second marriages.

Inviting children

A question that can arise when couples are compiling their guest list is whether or not to invite children. If you have children of your own, see page 76 for suggestions on how to include them on the day. While some people are happy to invite other people's children, some are worried that they might disrupt the proceedings. The main reasons why people do not invite children are:

- they take up space on the guest list and thus limit the numbers of adults the couple can invite
- small children may get bored and may make noise during the ceremony
- their parents may find it hard work keeping them entertained during a long sit-down meal.

However, there are various solutions to these problems. You could:

- choose not to invite any children
- invite them only to the reception, in which case you should make this plain on the invitations
- provide entertainment and care for the children at the reception venue (see page 196), and perhaps during the ceremony as well
- invite only children of very close friends and relatives, or those with whom you have a particularly close link – godchildren, for instance – and exclude others. You will need to make some tactful explanations to friends whose children are not included, but people are usually understanding of the problems.

If you decide not to invite children, you should leave the children's names off invitations, but follow-up with a phone call, or enclose a brief note, explaining the situation. Think about what you will say if anyone asks you to make an exception. Give parents plenty of warning so that they have time to make childcare arrangements.

The wedding invitations

The style of invitation you send out will set the tone for your wedding. A huge range of styles is available, and you can either buy them already printed (with space for you to fill in your details) from department stores and stationers, or order your own from specialist printers or stationery design companies. Look in the *Yellow Pages* or at the small ads in wedding magazines, then ring or visit one or two and ask to see samples of their work and a price list. Bear in mind that an ordinary printer can usually turn round invitations far faster than a specialist wedding stationer who operates through a department store or by mail order.

Another option is to make your own stationery. For printed invitations, you can use wedding software (page 67), or a desk-top publishing program. Another possibility is to handwrite your invitations. Either way, you can personalise them with, for example,

---

We decided not to invite children

When Julia married Tom they were both in their forties, and almost all of their friends had children, ranging in age from 3 to 15. Julia explained why they decided not to ask any children.

'I am very close to many of the children, but we wanted to sit down in a lovely restaurant with all our best friends and have a really good meal. The food was expensive and not the sort children usually like to eat, but more importantly we knew kids would just get bored. Space was limited as well, so for each child we asked we would have had to leave out one of our friends.

'I was concerned that people would be upset or offended, or might even not come at all, so before sending any invitations I rang every friend with children and explained what we were doing and said I hoped they would understand and that it wouldn't be a problem. Most friends said they would actually prefer to come without children because then they would be able to relax and enjoy themselves more easily, and because I gave plenty of notice most people were able to make arrangements for the children to be looked after. One or two people tried to persuade us to make an exception but we had already decided not to do that. Unfortunately, my cousin and her husband decided not to come because they couldn't bring their children.

'I would advise anyone to invite children only if that's what they really want to do. If not, be sensitive to your friends' feelings, speak to them personally and explain, but be very firm and stick by your decision.'

---

decorative card, tissue, ribbon, sequins. For inspiration, look at bridal magazines, or check out the suggestions for making your own invitations on *www.confetti.com*.

For a formal wedding, the invitations should be printed or engraved on good-quality white or cream card. The format is an upright, folded card measuring 14×18cm (5½×7in). Traditionally, invitations are engraved, which gives the lettering an embossed appearance, but this is expensive because a printing plate has to be made. Thermographic printing is cheaper and produces a similar result but does not look quite as smart. Flat printing is the least expensive option and produces lettering like that of a good computer printer. The print on invitations is usually black, but you could choose silver.

Quantity

You will need one invitation for each family or individual on your guest list. Etiquette demands that you also send one to the groom's parents, very close friends or relatives whom you already know will not be able to attend, the best man, attendants, and the minister and spouse (although they are unlikely to come to the reception unless they are also friends of the family). Add on another 20 or so to allow for any mistakes you may make while writing them and for any extra guests you may invite after the first replies have come in.

When to order

You will need to order your invitations at least four months in advance. This is because they take about two to four weeks to be printed and you may have to correct any mistakes the printer might make. Traditionally, invitations are sent out six to nine weeks before the wedding, but many couples send them out earlier. Giving a deadline for a reply is useful for deciding whether or not to send out any further invitations after the first batch of replies has been received.

Wording

Work out what you want the invitations to say, then give the printer a typed sheet with the wording exactly as you want it to appear. Guests are expected to reply formally, but it can be helpful to enclose a pre-printed reply card for them to return. When you write the invitations, think carefully about how to address each guest. With formal invitations, use each person's title rather than any familiar name by which you know them, e.g. 'Mr Jack Smith' rather than 'Uncle Jack'. For informal invitations, you can address people in whatever way you choose.

Formal weddings

The traditional wording for a very formal wedding is as follows:

Mr and Mrs Mark Baxter
request the pleasure of your company/
request the honour of your presence
at the marriage of their daughter
Alice
to Mr Edward Holland
at St Mary's Church, Lymington
on (day, date, month, year)
at (time)
and afterwards at
(reception location)

RSVP
(parents'/hosts' address)

Slightly less formal, but more commonly used, is this wording:

Mr and Mrs Mark Baxter
request the pleasure of the company of
(Name of guest(s) filled in by hand)
...
at the marriage of their daughter
Alice

If the bride's parents are divorced, if either is remarried or if one of them is deceased the same basic rule applies – the hosts send the invitation, and the announcement should make it clear how the hosts and bride are related to each other. In some situations, for instance where the bride's mother has remarried and changed her name, it is helpful to include the bride's surname as well. Some alternative wordings that follow the traditional style are given below:

The bride's mother as host, when the bride's father is deceased:

Mrs David Lloyd
requests the pleasure of your company
at the marriage of her daughter

The bride's father as host, when the bride's mother is deceased:

Mr David Lloyd
requests the pleasure of your company
at the marriage of his daughter

If the bride's mother is divorced she uses her forename, Mrs Katherine Lloyd; if remarried she uses her new husband's name, Mrs James Wallace.

The bride's divorced parents as hosts, where neither has remarried:

Mr David Lloyd and Mrs Katherine Lloyd
request the pleasure of your company
at the marriage of their daughter

The bride's divorced parents as hosts, where the mother has remarried:

Mr David Lloyd and Mrs James Wallace
request the pleasure of your company
at the marriage of their daughter

The bride's mother and stepfather as hosts:

Mr and Mrs James Wallace
request the pleasure of your company
at the marriage of her daughter

The bride's father and stepmother as hosts:

Mr and Mrs David Lloyd
request the pleasure of your company
at the marriage of his daughter

The bride as host:

Miss Sally Lloyd
requests the pleasure of your company
at her marriage to

The bride and groom as hosts:

Mr Adam Jackson and Miss Sally Lloyd
request the pleasure of your company
at their marriage

Continental Europeans and members of the practising Jewish community send cards with the names of both sets of parents:

Mr and Mrs John Collins
request the pleasure of
your company at the marriage
of their daughter
Anna
to Matthew, son of Dr and Mrs Owen

For a blessing service following a civil wedding, invitations should read as follows:

Mr and Mrs John Collins
request the pleasure of your company
at the Blessing of the Marriage
of their daughter
Anna

For an invitation to the reception only, the wording is:

Mr and Mrs John Collins
request the pleasure of your company
at the Reception to celebrate the marriage
of their daughter Anna

You could include a note explaining that due to the size of the ceremony venue only a limited number of guests can be accommodated.

Informal weddings

Invitations still come from the hosts, whether the bride's family or the couple themselves, but you have a wider choice of what to say and how to say it. You can be freer with design as well and could include a sketch of the wedding venue, a photograph of yourselves, a poem or quotation or any other means you choose to personalise your invitations.

Typical wording, where the bride's parents are hosts, would read like this:

Mr and Mrs John Collins
invite you/have much pleasure in inviting you
to the marriage of their daughter
Anna
to Matthew Owen

If the bride and groom are hosts:

Anna Collins and Matthew Owen
(or Anna and Matthew)
invite you to their wedding

Invitation checklist

Before having your invitations printed, check whether the cost includes the envelopes. When you receive the proof, check that:

- the invitation is worded correctly
- the lines break in the right places
- the day of the week and the date match
- all the names, including those of people and venues, are spelled correctly
- the address is complete and correct
- the punctuation is correct
- the style of lettering and the type of paper are the ones you chose.

Overnight guests

Some guests may have travelled a long way and need to stay overnight. If you are holding your reception at a hotel you may be able to arrange a deal and book several rooms at a reduced cost for these guests. Otherwise, seek out reasonable accommodation within easy reach of the venues and either offer to book for your guests or send them details so that they can make their own arrangements. This information could be included on your own website, if you have one (see page 68). *The Guide to Good Hotels, The Which? Pub Guide* and *The Good Bed and Breakfast Guide* all provide information about accommodation in your area.

Sending the invitations

Include clear directions and/or a map showing how to get to the wedding venue and from there to the reception. If necessary, these should be tailor-made for guests travelling from different directions. Do not enclose a wedding gift list but wait for people to ask for one to be sent. Send one invitation per family (unless the children are living away from home, say at university, in which case they should have one each) and write the names of those invited on the top left-hand corner of the invitation or fill in the space provided. Parents should assume that the invitation is for them alone if the children's names are not included.

Q *Can I use labels printed by my computer to send the invitations?*
A Yes, unless the wedding is very formal, in which case the envelopes should be handwritten, with the correct full name and rank or title of the guest.

Postponing the wedding

Occasionally circumstances demand that the wedding be delayed. You do not need to return wedding gifts if the wedding is postponed to a future date. Cards should be sent to guests telling them of the

Tip

A 'wedding book', signed by all your guests, makes a good souvenir of the day. Books designed for this purpose are available in department stores, but you could use any book with blank pages.

postponement and giving details of the new date if it is known. For details of what to do if the engagement is broken and the wedding cancelled, see pages 16–17.

Suitable wording for a printed notification of postponement would read as follows:

Owing to the recent illness/death
of Mrs Collins' father
the wedding of her daughter
Anna
to Matthew Owen
at (venue, time)
on (date)
has been postponed
until (time)
on (date)

Guest checklist

Name	Address	Tel/mobile/email	No. in party	Invitation sent	Accepted	Refused

Chapter 10

Wedding gifts

As soon as you have sent out your invitations most people will start to ask you what you would like as a wedding gift. You can make out your own list, selecting gifts from different sources, or put the list with one or more stores. Of course, you don't have to have a list at all. You could leave the choice up to guests, and for a small wedding, or if you really feel that you already have everything you need, this could be a straightforward solution.

Traditionally, it's considered bad form to enclose details of the gift list with the invitation. It's certainly impolite to print details of the gift list on the invitation itself, but many people do enclose a note giving details, or send a card from the store where the list is held.

Making your own list

One way to draw up a list is to browse round a number of different shops, picking out items you would like to receive. Draw up an informative list, including details of size, colour, manufacturer, model number and price. Include delivery instructions against any large items. If you are having your own wedding website (see page 68), then the easiest way to deal with the list is to post it on to the site. Guests can then look at it online, make their choice, and email you to tell you what they've chosen. You will need to keep the list up to date. Failing this, there are various other methods. The bride's mother, the couple or even the groom's mother could take charge of the list. When guests ask to see it, send the master copy with a stamped addressed envelope and ask them to cross off the item they choose and return the list or send it on. This method is cumbersome but does avoid duplication. A quicker method is to have several copies of the list and send one to any guest who asks. You may end up with some duplication but the whole process is speeded up and there is no danger of the list getting stuck with one person who then holds everyone else up. To make life easier, ask guests to ring whoever is in charge of the list, and tell them what they have chosen.

Putting your list with a store

Many couples place their list with one or two department stores, either in their home town or in a chain with branches nationwide, such as Argos or Marks & Spencer. Another option is to use an independent wedding list service, or an online wedding gift registry (see page 236), which will give you a far greater range of choice and make the whole process easier.

Wedding list departments are often very busy, and you might need to contact them as much as six months before the wedding, to make an appointment for a date two to three months ahead of time, when you will actually draw up the list. Ask about the store's policy on returns and exchanges. Check out the various ways in which guests can order. Will they have to go the store, which could be inconvenient for some, or can they order online, or over the phone?

When the time comes to draw up the list, allow plenty of time to browse round the store and choose items to put on your list. Have a think about the kind of things you want before you go. To draw up the list, you will usually either go through a catalogue, or go round the store, noting descriptions, sizes, colour, price and code. Some stores will produce copies of the list for you to send out, others keep a master list which guests can consult in person, over the phone, by

---

Gift list considerations

- List more items than there are guests, otherwise the last people to see the list will not have a choice.
- Choose items across the price range so that every guest can buy something within his or her means.
- Don't worry if some of the items you have chosen are very expensive as some people like to join up with friends and buy something more expensive than they could afford as an individual.

fax, or online. The store keeps track of who has ordered what, and you will be kept notified.

You could put a list at more than one store, choosing one for household, practical gifts and another for more decorative or specialised items. Some stores offer incentives, such as gift vouchers or discounts, if you place your list with them, but make sure they also offer a good delivery service and wide price range before you accept any incentive.

Delivery

Before you set up your list, ask how the gifts will be delivered to you. In some stores guests simply buy their gift and take it home ready to send to you or bring on the day. Other stores will deliver the gifts to you as they are purchased or will keep them all and deliver them after the wedding, notifying you of who has bought what in the meantime. Book a delivery date when you make out your list.

Q *Can I exchange a gift that I don't like?*

A If the same item is accidentally purchased twice or if you change your mind after receiving the gift, most stores will exchange it for something of the same value provided the item has not been used. Check on this before placing your list.

Compiling a wedding list

Couples who are setting up home for the first time will not need any help in drawing up a long list of things they need. Wedding magazines and websites (page 233) are a great source of inspiration. Leave yourselves plenty of time as choosing the right items for every part of the house takes a lot of thought, and the list needs to be ready about seven to ten weeks before the wedding.

The question of gifts is harder for the high percentage of couples who have lived together before marriage or who have been married before, as they already have most household items. So, if you are past the stage of needing saucepans and cutlery, here are a few suggestions:

- replace everyday items with luxurious versions: linen sheets, Egyptian cotton towels, top-of-the-range saucepans or kitchen knives
- decorative items: pictures, plants, cushions, antiques
- vintage wines
- luxury food items
- CDs or videos
- sports equipment
- plants for your garden
- tickets to a show or for travel
- gift vouchers for a specified store
- cash is increasingly acceptable as a gift suggestion
- unit trusts, shares, Premium Bonds
- donations to a specified charity.

Thank-you letters

Write a letter of thanks as each gift arrives; if you let them accumulate the task becomes far more daunting. Keep an up-to-date list (see opposite) and make a note when the thank-you letter has been sent. You should send a handwritten letter for every gift you receive, even if you have already thanked the giver in person. Some gifts will be received on, or after, the day. Send thank-you letters for these as soon as you return from honeymoon.

The letter need not be long but should be specific about the gift so that if, for instance, the store has delivered the wrong number of bowls the person concerned can put things right. If you are given money or vouchers, tell the giver how you plan to use them.

For gifts given jointly by two or three people, write to each one separately. A present given by a large group of people such as work colleagues needs only one letter, addressed to the group as a whole.

Displaying the gifts

The custom of displaying the wedding gifts is becoming less common. If you do decide on a display, make sure the reception venue has somewhere secure, preferably out of sight of public areas, where the gifts can be shown. Group similar items, such as glasses,

Gift checklist

Name of guest	Gift list sent	Gift received	Thank-you letter sent

linen etc. together, although if two items are nearly identical it is more tactful to place them apart. Cheques should be acknowledged by placing cards on the display table saying 'Cheque from Mr and Mrs John Smith'. You should not state the amount.

You will probably receive a number of gifts on the wedding day. Make sure that you have a safe place to put these and detail one of the bridesmaids to be responsible for keeping labels and cards with the gifts to which they belong. See Chapter 21 for details of how to make sure your wedding gifts are protected wherever they are.

Chapter 11

Wedding outfits

What you, the best man, ushers and attendants wear will depend on the wedding venue and how formal/informal your ceremony is going to be.

The bride

Choosing an outfit in which you will look and feel right on the day is one of the most important, enjoyable decisions you will make in the run-up to the ceremony. You don't need to stick to a traditional white dress, as there are lots of other options. There's plenty to inspire you: check out bridal magazines, the Internet (page 234), photographers' windows and advertisements for ideas. Don't go shopping with a lot of preconceptions. Many dresses look better on than off, so take time to try on a lot of styles.

Traditional wedding dresses

Buying

You can buy your wedding dress from any number of specialist bridal shops or department stores. Start your hunt early. Most bridal stores and departments stock samples only, and your dress will be ordered specially and could take between 12 and 16 weeks to arrive. You should also allow some time on top of this for any alterations that then have to be made.

When you shop, it is a good idea to make an appointment with a dress shop. Do this as far in advance as you can, and try to avoid Saturdays, as this is when popular shops can get booked up for several months ahead. Appointments usually last about an hour, and are with a fitter who can help you to get dresses on and off, and can find the accessories to go with them. You should have time to try on up to 15 dresses.

For a cheaper alternative, try high-street chains such as Monsoon and Bhs, for both traditional bridal dresses and evening gowns. Many evening dresses could readily be worn by a bride (or might suit an adult bridesmaid), and they often cost far less than a 'proper' wedding dress. Wear make-up and arrange your hair in a similar style to the one you would like to have on the day so you can get a good idea of how the dress will really look. Ask someone whose opinions you trust to go with you.

Tip

If you can shop well in advance of your wedding day you might be able to pick up an end-of-season bargain, for example you could buy an end-of-season summer dress in the autumn to wear the following summer. Most shops bring in new ranges once or twice a year and sell off the remains of previous ranges. These sales are often advertised in local newspapers.

Buying secondhand

Look in the *Yellow Pages*, in the small ads in wedding magazines for shops that specialise in secondhand gowns or on websites (page 234). Many dresses are sold privately through advertisements in local newspapers or specialist advertisements-only magazines such as *Loot*. Expect to pay about half of what the dress originally cost. Some dresses are sold unworn, and the rest may have been worn only once.

Having a dress made

Having a dress made will not necessarily be cheaper than buying a ready-made one – unless you can persuade a dressmaking friend or relative to make it for you – but you are more likely to get exactly what you want, and the dress will be made to fit you rather than being a 'standard' dress size (an important consideration if you fall between sizes or you are particularly short or tall, for example). Excluding the cost of the fabric, you can expect to pay from £250 for having a simple style made up, to as much as £3,000 for a very elaborate confection with a lot of fine detail which has to be sewn by hand.

Finding a dressmaker

If you know someone who wore a made-to-measure dress that you admired, finding out who their dressmaker was is probably the best starting point – not least because if that dressmaker is already fully booked, she (or he) should know of other dressmakers for you to contact. If you do not have any personal recommendations, try the *Yellow Pages* (under 'Dressmakers' and possibly 'Wedding services'). Alternatively, look in the small ads section at the back of wedding magazines and also the bridal magazines published by pattern companies such as Vogue, Butterick, Simplicity and so on. For a small fee, Butterick★ (of which Vogue Patterns is a subsidiary) can supply a list of dressmakers in your area – or go to www.sewbridal.co.uk. Other pattern companies may offer a similar service.

If you have Internet access, you can also find a designer or dressmaker in your area by using the Designer Directory★.

Getting the best from your dressmaker

When you find a dressmaker who seems suitable, ask to see examples of her (or his) work. If you are happy with what you see and the dressmaker is willing to take you on, you should arrange a meeting to talk about what you want. Take along pictures of the kind of dresses and accessories that you particularly like. These will give the dressmaker an idea of your likes and dislikes, which will, in turn, help her (or him) to come up with suitable designs for you. Before the first meeting it is also well worth your while visiting the off-the-peg wedding dress shops to try on dresses, veils and headdresses so that you get a good feel for what suits you (and what does not).

The next step will be for your dressmaker to show you a selection of sketches based on the ideas you discussed at the first consultation. If you like them and you feel comfortable about working with the dressmaker in what are going to be quite intimate situations, the next thing you need to know is how much it is going to cost. If, on the other hand, the sketches bear no relation to your dream dress and you feel that the dressmaker has not listened to any of your ideas, this may be the time to look for someone else: you will not feel your best on your wedding day if you have been bullied into wearing something that doesn't really suit you.

> **Tip**
>
> Long trains can be cumbersome at the reception, so if you are hav-
> ing a train, make sure it is detachable so it can be removed after the
> ceremony. Some dresses have a loop fixed on to the train so that
> the bride can hook it over her wrist and prevent it from trailing on
> the ground.

What will it cost?

The two main influences on the final cost of your dress are the fabric and your dressmaker's time. Clearly, the more fabric involved
and the more expensive it is, the costlier the final dress will be. How
much your dressmaker's time will cost depends on how elaborate
the design is, whether it involves a lot of intricate hand sewing and
how many fittings are necessary. The final cost will also be influ-
enced by the number of times you change your mind about what
you want, which is why many dressmakers can be reticent about
putting a price on their work until it is completed – although most
will be able to give you a rough guide.

If the estimated price sounds reasonable, you will need to agree
(preferably in writing):

* exactly what the dressmaker is supplying – just the dress, for
  example, or the dress and other accessories
* the delivery date
* dates for fittings
* a schedule for payments – whether you will pay a deposit and
  make a final payment, for example, or whether you will need to
  make interim payments as well (which may be the case if some
  special detail, such as hand embroidery or covered buttons, is
  subcontracted)
* who will pay for the fabric – this is usually the customer,
  although the dressmaker will usually supply routine haberdashery such as thread, binding, zips and so on
* whether VAT is payable and, if it is, whether it is included in the
  quoted price.

Choosing the fabric

Be guided by your dressmaker's specialist knowledge when it comes to choosing the material for your dress: she (or he) will know which fabrics are best suited to achieving the look you want. She (or he) will also know the best sources of bridal fabrics at competitive prices – shops specialising in bridal fabric can be in the most unexpected places and are rarely to be found on the high street. If you have a particular fabric in mind, your dressmaker can also advise you on which styles will work best (make sure that you take a sample of it to your first meeting).

Making it fit

Before your first fitting, it is a good idea to buy your wedding underwear and, once you have the fabric to match them to, your shoes. Getting the right underwear is particularly important for very close-fitting styles and having the shoes is vital for getting the length right. A good dressmaker is unlikely to cut the fabric until she (or he) has fitted you for a 'toile' (a test garment usually made out of cotton). Depending on your chosen style, subsequent fittings may involve getting component parts right so don't expect to see the final product until quite late on in the process.

Having a dress altered to fit

A dressmaker can also alter an existing dress to fit you. You might need to have this done if you have bought a secondhand or off-the-peg dress that doesn't fit you exactly or if you want to wear your mother's or grandmother's dress, for example.

Having a dress altered is also worth considering if you are on a tight budget, especially if you have an eye for a bargain and you manage to pick up a nearly suitable dress in the sales or in a second-hand or charity shop.

Making your dress yourself

If you have little or no experience of dressmaking but are drawn to the idea of making the dress yourself because you are on a tight budget, you should consider the following practicalities before making up your mind:

- **have you got a sewing machine?** If not, don't assume that you will be able to borrow one unless you have a firm offer of a loan

- **have you worked out what the material will cost?** It may be that once you have added up the cost of the dress fabric, other material for linings, petticoats, stiffening and haberdashery, you will find that it is not quite as cheap as you thought it was going to be
- **where are you going to cut it out?** You need a large, level, scrupulously clean surface (not carpet) to cut out a long frock accurately
- **where are you going to sew it?** You need somewhere that is well-lit, clean and preferably away from anything that could get spilt on the dress – so the kitchen table is not ideal
- **how are you going to alter it to fit?** Unless you have the help of another person or a tailor's dummy, it will be very difficult to get a good fit on your own
- **do you have a full-length mirror?** Fitting will be nearly impossible if you have not
- **are you familiar with pattern instructions?** It might be an idea to look through the instruction sheets of a wedding dress pattern before you commit yourself. Even if you have to buy the pattern to do this, it will be cheaper than possibly ruining a lot of expensive material
- **do you have back-up?** Unless you have a friend or relative who is willing to help out and/or advise you when you hit a tricky patch or make a mistake, it is probably not a good idea to tackle the job
- **could you make the bridesmaids' dresses instead?** This could be a good compromise because the dresses will be less crucial and, especially if you are having young children as your bridesmaids, more manageable to make.

If you decide that your wedding dress is something you can tackle and you have someone who will help if the need arises, it would be

---

Tip

After the wedding you can have your dress expertly cleaned and packed in acid-free tissue. Materials are also available to do the packing yourself. Some companies sell special boxes and tissue – complete with instructions on how to pack the dress away properly. Look in bridal magazines for addresses.

---

a good idea to invest in one or more of the special bridal magazines published by pattern companies. Not only will they have suitable patterns, but you will also find that they have addresses both of shops selling bridal fabrics and companies which sell fabric (often more cheaply) by mail order.

If, having considered the practicalities, you decide that it would not be a good idea to start practising your sewing skills on your wedding dress, there are still several options open to you – such as borrowing, hiring, having a dress altered or buying secondhand.

Hiring

Hiring is a less popular option than it used to be but it is still possible from some department stores or specialist shops. If you are having a themed wedding, you may be able to hire a dress in the appropriate style from a costume-hire company. You will need to give about 12 weeks' notice and should be able to collect the dress a couple of days before the wedding for return two days after. Check:

- that the dress will be available on your wedding day (get this in writing)
- that minor alterations are possible
- that the fee includes insurance against damage and cost of cleaning
- how many days the hire cost covers
- what alternatives are on offer if the dress is unavailable for any reason.

Veils, headdresses and hats

Veils vary in price depending on the length, amount of decoration and type of fabric, which might be silk or nylon tulle, lace or organza. The general rule is that if your dress has a train you wear a full-length veil, which falls to the ground and is about a foot longer than your train. Otherwise, you can have a short, face-framing veil, one that skims your shoulders or reaches to your fingertips, and it can be worn piled high on a headdress or falling simply from a band or tiara. Try on a range of styles with your chosen dress and remember that how you wear your hair on the day can alter the look significantly.

A headdress can be worn with or without a veil. Once again, bridal websites, magazines and shops will supply plenty of ideas, from simple circlets and Alice bands to tiaras. Floral headdresses are also popular (see page 108). You might prefer to wear a hat rather than a veil, in which case you could choose not to carry a bouquet.

Shoes

In winter white or pale-coloured shoes may be hard to come by outside specialist bridal shops, so buy them in spring or summer if you can. Shoes can be dyed or covered to get an exact match for your dress. Make sure the shoes are comfortable as well as stylish, since you will be on your feet for the greater part of the day. Very high heels can be hard to cope with under a full-length dress, especially if you are not used to them. Wear the shoes round the house so that they ease to the shape of your foot, and rub the soles with sandpaper or a metal-bristled suede brush to make sure there is no danger of slipping.

Underwear

Choose a well-fitting bra in a flesh tone and try it on with your dress to ensure that neither the bra nor straps can be seen. Wear the bra for a few hours before the day to make sure it is really comfortable. Tights or stockings will fit better if they have been washed once, and are less likely to ladder. Buy two pairs just in case one is laddered as you put it on.

Other accessories

Make sure your car hire includes a white umbrella so that you can get into church in the dry if it rains. Shawls, wraps, coats and cloaks can all be an integral part of your wedding outfit. Gloves may fit with your style of wedding dress but remember that your left hand needs to be uncovered during the ceremony. Jewellery can look good, but don't overdo it. You do not have to carry a bouquet.

Tip

Ask the chief bridesmaid or your mother to carry an emergency repair kit containing tiny safety pins, needle and thread, spare tights, headache pills, tissues, plaster, glasses or contact lens solutions, comb and make-up.

Outfits for a civil wedding

If you are marrying at alternative premises, such as a hotel or stately home, you can wear traditional bridal dress.

Alternatively, choose a dress or suit with skirt or trousers. You can opt for pastel colours, cream or ivory but there is no reason why you shouldn't wear a stronger colour if that's what suits you best. You could also wear a hat. If you have decided to have a themed wedding to suit the surroundings you could wear a dress to fit with the theme.

What to wear for a beach wedding

- Tight-fitting garments will feel uncomfortably hot. Choose light-weight cotton or crêpe de chine fabrics in a loose style.
- Open sandals or bare feet are most comfortable, so don't forget the pedicure. Enclosed shoes will make your feet hot and likely to swell, and heels will sink into the sand.
- Pack your outfits carefully with plenty of tissue paper and carry as hand luggage. Hang them in a steamy bathroom for 15 minutes on arrival to let the creases drop out.

Going-away outfits

This is the outfit you will wear to leave the reception, although if you have a very lavish wedding dress and a long reception with dancing you could change earlier in the evening so that you can dance in comfort. Otherwise, the choice is yours and you can wear a dress, a suit or something more casual. What you wear can depend on where you are going after the reception. If you are flying off on honeymoon that day then comfortable clothes in uncrushable fabrics that will suit the climate of your destination are the obvious choice. If, however, you are spending a night at a hotel you can choose a dressy outfit that will look good in photographs as you leave but which can be worn again in future.

The groom

For a very formal church wedding the groom usually wears morning dress or a suit. The couple's fathers, the best man and the ushers should wear the same style of dress as the groom.

Traditional morning dress consists of a black or grey three-piece suit with tail coat, or black tail coat with grey pinstripe trousers and a grey waistcoat. The morning dress is worn with a wing-collared shirt and cravat, or an ordinary collar and tie. Make sure all the men in the wedding party know exactly what combination you have chosen so they can all wear the same.

You can choose a patterned or coloured cravat, waistcoat or cummerbund, which might pick up a colour from the bride's bouquet or the bridesmaids' dresses. Morning dress is extremely expensive to buy, and most men choose to hire it. Go to a reputable company well in advance for a fitting. Expect to pick it up a couple of days in advance and arrange for it to be returned within two days after the wedding.

Check whether cleaning is included in the price. All the accessories will also be available for hire. These include grey gloves, which traditionally are carried, not worn, and a silk top hat, which is worn only for some of the photographs. You can also hire tiepins or cufflinks, but most men prefer to use their own. Wear a pair of comfortable and smart black shoes.

As well as formal morning dress, hire outlets have a wide range of other possibilities for less formal church or civil weddings. Look at websites (page 234) for ideas. Possibilities include Nehru jackets, Highland wear, evening dress and designer suits. Many men wear a smart suit with two or three pieces. Colour and style are entirely your choice. If you are wearing a dark suit, you could wear a colourful tie, shirt or waistcoat. The best man should also wear a suit, which should complement the groom's outfit but need not be an exact match.

If you are getting married on a beach abroad, there's no need for jacket or tie. Trousers or shorts in cotton or linen, worn with a cool shirt, would be fine.

The bridegroom can leave the reception wearing the same suit he wore for the wedding, or if he wore morning dress he can change into a jacket and tie with smart trousers or perhaps just a shirt and casual trousers.

Bridesmaids and page boys

The first decision you need to make is whether to buy, hire or make the outfits. They could come from the same source as the bride's dress, or the adult bridesmaids may be happy to buy their own dresses off-the-peg from a department store or bridal shop. Decide on your budget and who will pay. Traditionally, the bride's family pay for the attendants' clothes, but bridesmaids or, if they are children, their parents, may be happy to contribute or bear the whole cost, particularly if you choose styles which can be worn again for parties. Make it clear when you ask them to be bridesmaids who is going to pay for their outfits.

Choosing a style

The bridesmaids' dresses could be similar to your wedding dress but not identical, for example if yours has a full skirt their dresses could be straight but with the same neckline or sleeves as yours. Alternatively, they could be almost identical in style but in a different colour and without some of the detail that yours might have.

The adult and young bridesmaids do not have to wear the same styles as each other. The older bridesmaids could wear straight or knee-length dresses while the younger ones wear dresses that are fuller in style or full-length. Other options could be to dress the children in a paler shade of the colour the adult bridesmaids are wearing, or make the older bridesmaids' dresses one solid colour and the smaller girls' dresses in a print, or in cream or ivory with trimmings in your chosen colour.

Page boys could wear velvet suits, smart trousers with waistcoat, sailor suits or Scottish outfits with kilt and sporran. Miniature morning suits for children are available to hire.

The bride's mother

At a formal wedding the bride's mother has an important and prominent role to play as hostess. Her outfit should be chosen so that it does not clash with the bride's colour scheme, and although her clothes should be attractive and eye-catching they should not draw attention away from the bride. It is advisable for her to confer with the groom's mother before shopping, so that they avoid wearing outfits that are too similar or that will not look good together in photographs. Large-brimmed hats can overshadow the face in pictures and cast unflattering shadows, so choose with care.

Chapter 12

Flowers

To find a suitable florist, look in the *Yellow Pages* or local newspapers, or consult wedding magazines and websites (page 233). Sometimes photographers or hairdressers have free leaflets listing local companies that offer wedding services, but probably the best source is personal recommendation. Most florists have a portfolio of their wedding designs.

As florists are always very busy during the summer, you should book well in advance, although you won't be able to plan in detail until you have chosen your outfit and colour scheme. Arrange to meet the florist a couple of months before the wedding to go through the arrangements and make some firm decisions.

The initial meeting

- Take with you any **inspirational pictures** you have collected. Even if the flowers in a bouquet you admire are difficult to get hold of at the time of year you are getting married, the florist should be able to achieve a similar effect using different flowers.
- Take **swatches of fabric from your dress** and the bridesmaids' outfits if possible, plus sketches or photographs of the styles. These will help the florist to suggest a style of bouquet to suit your dress.
- Any **colour or combination of colours is acceptable**, but if you choose white flowers be careful, as it can be hard to match the shade with that of your dress. For example, a bluish-white dress would make creamy flowers look drab and discoloured.
- Work out **how much you want to spend on your flowers** so you can give the florist an idea of the size of your order. You should also have given some thought to how many buttonholes

and corsages you need and where you would like flowers in the wedding venue and at the reception.

Which flowers?

Although most flowers are now available all year round (thanks to hothouse production) they are always more expensive out of season. Many flowers have traditional meanings, which you might like to take into account when making up your bouquet. Several of the flowers listed opposite, such as chrysanthemums and roses, are available across several seasons.

The bouquets

Hand-tied bouquets are popular and vary in style, depending on the shape and size and choice of flowers and foliage. They are very striking but can be heavy and cumbersome. Other options include a more formal wired bouquet; a posy, which is rounded in shape; or a single flower.

Keep the style of your dress in mind when choosing your bouquet. Bodice detail may be hidden if it is behind a large bouquet, and you might prefer an arrangement that can be held in the crook of your arm. Shorter, simpler dresses call for smaller bouquets, while a tailored gown with a train can be just as beautifully offset by half a dozen lilies as by a more complex and sophisticated arrangement.

The bridesmaids' flowers should complement the bride's bouquet and are usually smaller posies made from the same flowers. Very young bridesmaids may tire of holding a bouquet, so you could give them a ball of flowers on a ribbon (pomander) or flowers in small baskets to carry; these can both be looped over the arm.

Floral headdresses

Floral headdresses – in the form of a circlet or coronet – are an attractive alternative to tiaras, circlets or Alice bands. Flowers can also be attached to a hair band, wired or even woven into your hair. Ask your florist's advice on which varieties to use, as some wilt far more readily than others. All fresh flowers are susceptible to heat, and may lose their freshness as the day wears on. Try to handle them as little as possible while your hair is being arranged.

Seasonal flowers and their meanings

Spring
apple blossom	good luck in the future
camellia	perfect loveliness
carnation	deep love
daffodil	regard
daisy	innocence
honeysuckle	devotion
iris	burning love
jasmine	grace
lily	purity
mimosa	sensitivity
tulip	love
white lilac	youthful innocence

Summer
cornflower	hope
lily of the valley	renewed happiness
rose	love, happiness
red rose	I love you
white rose	I am worthy of you
sweet pea	delicate pleasures

Autumn
red chrysanthemum	I love you
white chrysanthemum	truth
gypsophila	fertility
orchid	beauty

Winter
snowdrop	hope
ivy	fidelity

Flowers checklist

Name of florist	
Address	
Telephone/fax/email	
Contact	
Date booking made	
Confirmed in writing	

	Colour	Type of flowers	No.	Delivery details	Who pays?	Cost £
Bride's bouquet						
Bridesmaids' bouquets						
Adults						
Children						
Headdresses						
Bride						

Adult bridesmaids							
Child bridesmaids							
Buttonholes							
Groom							
Best man							
Ushers							
Couple's fathers							
Others							
Corsages							
Bride's mother							
Groom's mother							
Flowers in wedding venue							
Altar							
Pulpit							
Lectern							
Windowsills							
Font							

(continued overleaf)

Flowers in wedding venue (*continued*)	Colour	Type of flowers	No.	Delivery details	Who pays?	Cost £
Columns						
Entrance						
Chancel steps						
Pew ends						
Lych gate						
Chuppah						
Reception flowers						
Entrance						
Hanging baskets						
Pedestals						
Covered walkway						
Cake table						
Head table						
Buffet table						
Any other flowers						
VAT						
Total cost						

Preserving your bouquet

If you want to toss your bouquet into the crowd as you leave, you could extract one or two flowers first and ask someone to press them as a souvenir. There are also specialist companies who will preserve the whole bouquet in the form of a pressed picture (see page 236).

Buttonholes and corsages

Buttonholes are worn by all the men in the wedding party – groom, best man, the ushers and the couple's fathers. Traditionally, the men wear a white or cream carnation or rose, but you can choose any colour or flower you like to match those in your bouquet or pick up a shade from your colour scheme.

Corsages are worn by the mothers of the bride and groom and consist of two or three flowers and some foliage. Consult the wearers about their preferred colours and weight, because it may not be possible to attach a heavy corsage to a light silk outfit, for example, without damaging the fabric.

Flowers for a religious ceremony

You should discuss the church flowers with the minister when you first meet. Most will be happy for you to provide your own flowers (you might be able to ask the regular church flower arranger to do them for you in return for a contribution to the church funds), while others have a policy of supplying all the floral arrangements. Alternatively, you could make use of the flowers that have been arranged for the Sunday service or choose not to have any at all.

Where to put flowers for the ceremony

In church, with the minister's permission, you can place flowers in some or all of the following sites:

- altar (some ministers prefer to leave this bare so that the cross remains the focal point)
- pulpit
- lectern
- windowsills

- font (may not be allowed, particularly if there is a christening the following day)
- columns
- church entrance
- chancel steps
- pew ends
- lych gate.

In a synagogue, flowers may be used on the *chuppah*.

Often more than one wedding is held on the same day, making it impossible to change the flowers. If this is the case, the cost of the flowers is usually divided between couples, and you should all meet with the church helpers to discuss what type of flowers would best suit you all.

Flowers for a civil ceremony

Most register offices keep an arrangement of fresh flowers permanently on display. Ask at your first visit whether you can bring in flowers of your own, as policies vary. On a busy day, when one wedding follows quite rapidly after another, there may not be time to set up new flowers. If you are marrying at an approved licensed venue, such as a hotel or stately home, then you should be able to use as many flowers as you wish.

Flowers for the reception

Some reception venues include a number of floral arrangements as part of the overall cost. Check this when you are making your booking. Most will be happy for you to provide your own flowers. Alternatively, you may be able to arrange for the transport of your own large pedestal arrangements from the church for further display at the reception venue.

Where to put flowers at the reception

- at the entrance to the room
- elsewhere in the main room – on sills or side tables
- on the buffet table
- on each dining table, with a more elaborate arrangement for the top table. The main table could also be dressed with swags or garlands of flowers

- on top of the cake and on the cake table
- on pedestals around the room or marquee
- in hanging baskets if you are having a marquee
- spiralling up the columns of a marquee
- on the banisters.

You could either continue the floral theme from your bouquet and wedding venue or choose a totally different style, using other colours and flowers. If your florist is arranging the flowers at the reception, he or she will want to know:

- when the flower arrangers can have access to the reception venue
- if there is another booking immediately before or after yours and, if there is, when the flowers must be removed. One option could be for the people using the room after you to use your flowers and contribute to the cost
- (if you are using a marquee) the colour of the lining, whether or not it has poles or a covered walkway that need decorating and, if so, how many poles there are
- (if you are using a marquee) whether you want to use pedestals or have hanging baskets and how many of them you need. (The marquee company will need to provide rope to attach the hanging baskets.) The benefit of having hanging baskets is that although pedestals look beautiful to the first few guests who enter the room, if it is a stand-up reception, they will not be seen by many people once the room is full. Hanging baskets will be visible to everyone throughout the proceedings.

Chapter 13

Transport

Most people who have a formal white wedding hire at least one chauffeur-driven car and, more usually, two. Hired wedding cars are comfortable and roomy, allowing the bride to travel to the ceremony in style and with her dress uncrushed. The bride's mother and attendants, who travel together, leave the house first and wait for the bride in the church porch. The second car takes the bride and her father (or person giving her away) from the house to the church. It is up to the best man to arrange for the groom to arrive at the church in plenty of time (usually about 40 minutes before the ceremony).

After the ceremony, the bride and groom leave for the reception in one car, followed by the bride's parents and possibly the attendants in the second. You need to think through the transport arrangements well in advance to make sure that suitable transport is available for everyone. On the day it is the best man's job to make sure that everyone can get to the reception without difficulty.

For a small civil wedding the arrangements are less formal, and bride and groom can arrive together if they wish. You can use hire cars, private family cars or taxis.

Wedding cars

Hired cars are the most popular choice, and a wide variety are on offer, ranging from vintage Rolls-Royces and Daimlers, through American Cadillacs and stretch limousines, to open-topped E-type Jaguars. Personal recommendation is the best way to find a reliable hire company, otherwise you should try the *Yellow Pages*, wedding websites or a wedding magazine.

Book your transport well in advance and expect to pay at least £250, possibly substantially more for something unusual. Cars are usually decorated with white or cream ribbons, but if you want flowers or other decorations you may have to arrange these your-selves. When choosing the cars bear in mind that a white dress can look dull in front of a white car, and it may look better if you choose one in a darker colour such as maroon, navy blue or black. Many companies offer a complete package tailored to your requirements for the day.

Before you book:

- visit the company and see the cars for yourself
- ensure that the car you see is the one you will get, not a similar one or a different model. Confirm this in writing
- ask whether the car is a genuine vintage, i.e. made between 1917 and 1930, or veteran, which can either be pre-1916 or pre-1905. Cars made 'in the style of' older cars can look effective and should be cheaper to hire than an original
- inspect the general condition of the car: tyres, seating, wood-work, paintwork etc.
- ask if ribbons or flowers are included in the price
- check that a large umbrella in cream or white comes with the car
- the law requires you to wear a seatbelt in the front and back of a modern car, but vintage and veteran cars and some classic models have them in the front only or not at all. If the car was made before the seatbelt laws were enforced you are exempt from wearing them. This could be an important factor to con-sider if your dress is likely to be creased by a belt
- ask for written confirmation of the cars to be provided, date and times, whether a chauffeur is provided (and if so, what uniform he or she will wear), insurance cover and any extra charges
- the confirmation should include an assurance that the cars will be used only for your wedding on that date and not for any oth-ers on the same day. This is because you do not want to find that your car is late picking you up because it was delayed at a previ-ous wedding.

Borrowing cars

If you do not want to spend so much on transport, you could borrow suitable cars from family or friends, who might also be willing to act as chauffeur for you. Give the cars a thorough clean and polish and decorate them with ribbons and flowers. Make sure that there is room for you to get in and out comfortably in your wedding dress. Although open-topped cars sound attractive, the wind can wreak havoc with your hair and veil unless you travel exceptionally slowly.

Parking arrangements

Find out in advance what the parking regulations are at both the ceremony and reception venues, particularly if either is in a busy town. If no large car parks are available at the venue itself, check out other nearby car parks and include their details and perhaps a map with your invitations.

Other forms of transport

Horse-drawn carriages, with optional liveried coachmen and foot-men or pageboys, or closed carriages, with heated interiors for winter, are also available. Although romantic, they are feasible only if the journey is fairly short and does not include any steep hills. Book well in advance for these, as popular summer dates can be booked up as much as two years in advance. In an open carriage you will be at the mercy of the weather, so you need to be reasonably confident of a fine day. Most companies offer a choice of colour of the horses. Expect to pay between £400 and £800, depending on the distance, number of horses and the type of carriage.

Leaving the reception

Traditionally, it is up to the best man to ensure that the newly-weds have the means of transport to leave the reception. This may be the groom's own car, left at the reception venue earlier. If fun-loving guests or ushers decide to 'decorate' the car it is up to the best man to make sure that it is not damaged and any embellishments can be easily removed. You can use one of your hire cars again, particularly if the reception has been a short one, but a private car or taxi is probably more suitable, especially as the cost per hour of a hired car is high.

Couples wanting to leave their reception in style could consider:

- a hot-air balloon (only possible when the weather is calm, and exactly where you will land cannot be guaranteed)

- motorbike with side car
- tandem bicycle
- rickshaw
- boat, from a waterside reception
- black taxi cab.

Transport hire checklist

Name of hire company	
Address	
Telephone/fax/email	
Contact	
Date booking made	
Number of cars booked	
Other types of transport booked (horse and carriage etc.)	
Confirmed in writing	
Cost £	
Deposit £	
Balance due £	

Chapter 14

Music and readings for the ceremony

Adding carefully chosen music and readings is a way of making your ceremony more personal.

Civil ceremony

The key point to remember is that any music or reading included in a civil ceremony must be non-religious. For example, this means that you cannot have any version of 'Ave Maria' or 'Pie Jesu', or any extract from a mass or requiem, nor can you have readings from the Bible, the Koran, the Torah, or Gibran's 'The Prophet'. Many register offices will allow you to use your own music at the discretion of the superintendent registrar. Restrictions on space and the amount of time allowed for each wedding mean that you will almost certainly not be able to have live music, although you will probably be allowed to use your choice of recorded music for a few minutes before and after the ceremony.

Approved premises will generally be more flexible, but do check before booking if music is very important to you, as some hotels and country houses have fairly strict policies about the use of music during the ceremony. At approved premises it is often possible to arrange the ceremony to include a prelude, processional and recessional (see pages 122–3 and 126) and you may be able to use live or recorded music.

As to your choice of music, any of the non-religious pieces listed on pages 123–6 would be suitable. You can get inspiration from the many compilations of romantic and mood music, both classical and modern, which are widely available on CD from record stores and libraries. Among the most popular modern pieces played at civil weddings are:

- 'My Heart Will Go On' by Celine Dion
- 'The Miracle of Love' by the Eurythmics
- 'Your Song' by Elton John
- 'Stand By Me' by Ben E. King
- 'Love Me Tender' by Elvis Presley
- 'When A Man Loves A Woman' by Percy Sledge.

Readings

You may also be able to have one or more non-religious readings at a civil ceremony, again with the superintendent registrar's approval. These could be read by a family member or friend, or even by the bride or groom. Anthologies, such as *The Oxford Book of Marriage*, (Rubinstein, H (ed.), 1992, OUP), which may be available from libraries, are a useful source of suitable poems and prose. Once again, wedding websites (page 233) provide plenty of ideas and inspiration. Suggestions include:

- 'If ever two were one, then surely we . . .' by Anne Bradstreet
- 'How do I love thee? Let me count the ways . . .' (from *Sonnets from the Portuguese*) by Elizabeth Barrett Browning
- 'Never marry but for love . . .' by William Penn
- 'My heart is like a singing bird . . .' (from *A Birthday*) by Christina Rossetti
- 'Shall I compare thee to a summer's day? . . .' ('Sonnet 18') by William Shakespeare
- 'My true love hath my heart and I have his. . .' (from *Arcadia*) by Sir Philip Sidney.

Alternative ceremonies

If you choose to have an alternative ceremony (i.e. one that carries no legal weight but which is a celebration of your marriage that takes place after a civil ceremony) you are free to choose any readings and music you wish, with or without religious content. See pages 26 and 150–2 for more information on the content of alternative ceremonies.

121

Religious ceremony

Music creates a memorable atmosphere for your wedding ceremony and is used:

- before the bride arrives (the prelude)
- as she walks down the aisle (the processional)
- while the register is being signed
- as the married couple leave the church (the recessional).

Two or three hymns and perhaps a psalm are also usually sung during the service.

Discuss the music the first time you meet the minister. Most churches are equipped with an organ, and the organist will be able to suggest suitable pieces if you need some ideas. Bear in mind the organist's abilities and the quality of the organ when making a selection. You will usually have to pay between £50 and £80 if the church organist plays for you. A family member or friend who is an accomplished organist might be able to play at the ceremony instead.

You might like to have a choir to lead the singing during your service and perhaps sing a piece of your choice while you are signing the register. Some churches have their own choir, which you can hire for a small fee (probably no more than £100 and possibly less), but you could hire a professional choir or one from a local school instead.

The selection of pieces suitable for weddings is wide, and your local record library or shop should be able to provide some compilation recordings to help you choose. You do not have to restrict yourselves to religious pieces – but check that your minister has no objections before settling on something secular.

The prelude

The organist plays softly for about 20 minutes before the ceremony is due to start. The pieces should be calm and peaceful, setting the mood for the event and leading up to the exciting moment when the bride arrives. Most organists will be able to suggest a repertoire, but suitable pieces include:

- 'Sheep may safely graze' by J.S. Bach

- Moonlight Sonata (slow movement); Pathétique Sonata (slow movement) by Beethoven
- Symphony no. 6 (slow movement) 'From the New World' by Dvořák
- 'Nimrod' from *Enigma Variations* by Elgar
- *Water Music*; Pastoral Symphony from *Messiah* by Handel
- 'Gymnopédie no. 1' by Satie.

The processional

Joyful and stately music is played as the bridal party enter the church and continues as they process down the aisle. The pace should be steady, making it easy to walk slowly without feeling rushed. You might like to choose one of the following:

- 'Trumpet Voluntary' by Boyce
- 'Theme from the St Anthony Chorale' by Brahms
- 'Trumpet Voluntary' ('Prince of Denmark's March') by Clarke
- 'Arrival of the Queen of Sheba'; 'Minuet' from *Music for the Royal Fireworks* by Handel
- 'Bridal March' by Parry
- 'Bridal March' from *Lohengrin* by Wagner.

Hymns and psalms

It is usual to have three hymns or psalms during the ceremony, the first at the beginning of the service, the second after the marriage and the third after you have signed the register. You can have just two hymns or only one if you prefer. It is advisable to choose hymns that are well known, especially if the congregation is small or you are not using a choir. Below is a selection of well-known popular hymns often used at weddings:

- 'Come down, O Love divine'
- 'Glorious things of thee are spoken'
- 'Jerusalem'
- 'Love divine, all loves excelling'
- 'Praise my soul the King of heaven'
- 'The Lord's my shepherd' (to the tune Crimond)
- 'Lord of all hopefulness'
- 'I vow to thee my country'
- 'Dear Lord and Father of mankind'.

Suitable psalms, which may be said or sung, include:

- Psalm 37 ('Put thou thy trust in the Lord . . .')
- Psalm 67 ('God be merciful unto us and bless us . . .')
- Psalm 83 ('How lovely is Thy dwelling place, O Lord of Hosts! . . .')
- Psalm 128 ('Blessed are all they that fear the Lord . . .').

Signing the register

At this point in the proceedings a friend or relative could play a solo on a musical instrument or sing, or the church choir could sing a psalm or anthem. Another option would be to book professional instrumentalists or singers to perform, or arrange for a recorded piece to be played. Tell the minister which pieces you have chosen to ensure there is no objection. If you want to use recorded music, you must get permission to set up a sound system; make sure you leave enough time to test it properly and find someone competent to operate it. The same applies if you want to make a recording of the ceremony. You can choose from a wide range of classical, modern and popular instrumental arrangements and songs, such as:

- 'Adagio in G Minor' (orchestral recording or organ) by Albinoni
- 'Jesu, joy of man's desiring' (organ with or without choir or soloist) by J.S. Bach
- 'Flower Duet' from *Lakmé* (soloists) by Delibes
- 'Ave Maria' (choir or soloist) by Gounod
- 'Ave Maria' (organ or strings, with or without choir or soloist) by Schubert
- 'Exultate Jubilate'; 'Laudate Dominum' (soloist) by Mozart.

Tip

Performances that take place at wedding ceremonies and receptions – whether live or of recorded music – are deemed 'private', so you do not need to pay any copyright fees or obtain a public broadcast licence.

Order of service sheets

When you have made a final decision on the music and readings for your ceremony you can have order of service sheets printed, or design them yourself, see page 67. You will need to order one for each guest, plus a dozen extra. These should be placed at the church before the service, and it is the ushers' job to give one to each guest and to ensure that sheets are placed at the front of the church for the minister, bride and groom to use.

On the front of the service sheet the name of the church and the date and time of the ceremony appear in the centre of the page. The bride's name is printed in the bottom right-hand corner and the groom's in the bottom left-hand corner. Inside are printed all the verses of hymns, all the words of the prayers and responses, along with details of the music to be played. A printer will have a sample sheet on which you can base your layout, but you will need to provide a typed copy of the wording you want to use. Check this with the minister before going ahead with printing to ensure that all details are correct.

It is possible, though unlikely, that your chosen hymns will still be protected by copyright, in which case you will need to seek permission from the copyright holder to reprint the words in your order of service sheets. Details of this will be found in the hymn book, either in the acknowledgements at the front or under the paragraph on copyright. If permission is required, the relevant address will be shown in the hymn book. A few copyright holders ask for a reproduction fee, but most are happy with a brief printed acknowledgement.

You do not have to have printed order of service sheets. If you want to keep costs down you can use the service as laid out in a prayer book, and the congregation can sing from hymn books. Make sure that enough of these books are available for the ushers to distribute.

The recessional

This is the moment for a really joyful explosion of sound, as the newly married couple and their attendants leave the church. Traditional choices include:

- 'Toccata in G' by Dubois
- 'March no. 4' from *Pomp and Circumstance* by Elgar
- 'Wedding March' from *A Midsummer Night's Dream* by Mendelssohn
- 'Postlude in D' by Smart
- 'Fanfare' by Whitlock
- 'Toccata' from *Symphony No. 5* by Widor.

Bells

A glorious peal of bells enhances any traditional church ceremony. However, an increasing number of churches have only one bell, although they may be able to use a recorded peal. The bells can be rung before and after the ceremony, and the bellringers are paid in cash by the best man on the day. A peal of bells costs between £30 and £60.

Alice and Henry

Alice and Henry initially booked their wedding for 2.30pm, then changed the time to 2pm to fit in with their reception arrangements. Unfortunately the minister had made the change in his desk diary but had forgotten to make the change in the bellringers' book and the ringers turned up after the ceremony had started. Always double-check arrangements, especially if you make any changes.

Readings

Many people like to include one or two readings in their service, although this is not compulsory. Suitable readings from the Authorized Version of the Bible include:

- I Corinthians, Chapter 13 ('Love is patient and kind')
- Ecclesiastes 4, 9–12 ('Two are better than one')

- I John, Chapter 4, 7–12 ('Beloved, let us love one another')
- Ruth 1, 16–17 ('Whither thou goest, I will go')
- Song of Solomon 8, 6–7 ('Set me as a seal upon thine heart').

If you want a reading taken from any source other than the Bible, get your minister's agreement beforehand. There are many suitable poems that could be read, and more details are given on page 121.

Music checklist for ceremony

	Name of piece of music	Played by
Name of musician(s)		
Address		
Telephone/fax/email		
Details of booking		
Cost		
Confirmed in writing		
Name of piece of music		**Played by**
Prelude		
Processional		
Hymns		
Signing of the register		
Recessional		

Chapter 15

Wedding cake options

The traditional tiered wedding cake makes a grand centrepiece for the wedding feast and can take pride of place on a buffet table. At a sit-down meal the cake should be placed on a separate table where it can be seen by the guests but where it does not obscure their view of the bride and groom. Order the cake well in advance, as traditional rich fruit cake improves with age and should be made at least two months before icing.

The first question to consider is how many people the cake will have to serve. Remember to allow for those absent on the day (either because they couldn't come or because you weren't able to invite them). You can send them a piece after the wedding in special little boxes (available in department stores); if you wish, these can be printed with details of your wedding.

Also decide whether you want to keep the top tier for a future celebration, such as your first wedding anniversary or the christening of your first child, and remember to allow for this in your

No. portions needed	Shape	Size of tiers (allows for keeping top tier)
60	round, 2 tiers	25cm/10in, 15cm/6in
100	round, 3 tiers	28cm/11in, 18cm/7in, 12.5cm/5in
130–140	round, 3 tiers	30cm/12in, 20cm/8in, 15cm/6in
	square, 3 tiers	25cm/10in, 20cm/8in, 15cm/6in
160–180	round, 3 tiers	30cm/12in, 25cm/10in, 20cm/8in
	square, 3 tiers	28cm/11in, 23cm/9in, 18cm/7in
200–220	round, 4 tiers	30cm/12in, 25cm/10in, 20cm/8in, 15cm/6in
	square, 3 tiers	30cm/12in, 25cm/10in, 20cm/8in

calculations. You will need about 2.25kg/5lb of fruit cake for every 45 to 50 guests. Another way to estimate the size needed is by diameter of the cakes (see page 128).

Fruit cake, being very rich, is economical to serve as only small slices need be given. If you choose sponge cake instead you will get approximately half the number of servings per tier.

Using sponge cakes instead of fruit cakes

More and more people steer away from heavy fruit cakes, opting instead for vanilla or chocolate sponge. These cakes can be iced to look like a conventional cake and, if tiered, can be stacked or arranged using special pillars with interior rods, which go through the cake and rest on the stand beneath. These bear the weight of the cakes on top. Alternatively, sponge cakes can be frosted, or covered with rich ganache icing. However, if the weather is hot these finishes are likely to melt, so the cake must be displayed somewhere cool.

Tip

One way to keep costs down but still provide a spectacular centre-piece to the wedding meal is to have a cake which can double as dessert. A pyramid of chocolate-iced profiteroles, decorated with spun caramelised sugar, is ideal. Allow three buns per portion. You could also try a French croquembouche – a hillock of choux buns filled with flavoured creams, with caramel and spun sugar poured over – which is traditionally served at parties in France. A chocolate gâteau would be another good choice, or for a smaller gathering, a large Swiss roll, filled with cream and brandy-soaked glacé fruits, would look sumptuous and taste delicious.

Shapes and decorations

Square and round are the most popular shapes and can be arranged either on pillars or stacked, with the tiers resting on top of each other. Flower shapes, rectangles, octagons or horseshoes are other possibilities. A professional cake-maker would be able to produce a cake in any shape you want: a fairytale castle, an island, even a person.

White royal icing is the traditional choice, but fondant icing – being much softer – is easier to eat and gives you more scope for imaginative decoration as it can be moulded and modelled. Although white is the most common choice, the cake could be iced in a colour to fit in with the scheme of the flowers or bridesmaids' dresses.

The cake can be iced with swags, flowers, latticework or many other decorations. Professional confectioners will have a book of photographs showing all the different designs they offer. On top you can have a bride and groom model or a small arrangement of fresh flowers, which should be ordered with your other flowers. Silk flowers are a good alternative to fresh, or a skilled confectioner can make sugar flowers which can be kept as a souvenir. These add considerably to the cost, however, as they are very time-consuming to make.

Who will make the cake?

Making the cake yourself, or asking a family member or friend to do it, is a good way to save money. Ingredients for a simple three-tiered wedding cake (feeding 80–100 people) cost about £50 from a supermarket. Another way to keep costs down is to buy plain iced fruit cakes from a supermarket and construct your own tiered cake, which you can then have professionally decorated. Costs range from £10 to £30 per tier.

To make the cake yourself, start by baking it three months before the wedding. The tiers will probably have to be done in relays unless you have access to an extra-large oven. Once you have made the cakes, wrap them in greaseproof paper then in foil and store for at least two months in a cool, dry place until you are ready to ice them. Icing is a job best left to the professionals unless you are very experienced, and you should be able to take the cakes to a cake-decorator for icing and decoration four to six weeks before the wedding.

If you decide to have the cake made for you, consult the *Yellow Pages* for a suitable baker and confectioner. Shop around to compare prices and ask to taste a sample of a typical cake. Confirm all the details in writing when you order and remember to check:

- **when the cake will be delivered**
- **who will assemble it at the reception venue**. If you are using caterers they may do this or else the cake supplier will do it

- **how the cake will be packed**. Each tier should be boxed separately to avoid damage
- for a tiered cake, **whether the pillars and display tray are included in the price**
- if the top decorations are provided. Most confectioners will be able to offer you a wide choice
- **if the confectioner is insured against loss or damage of the cake prior to delivery or during transit**.

Tip

Storing the top layer is only possible if you choose a fruit cake, as sponge cakes do not keep for more than a few days. First you must strip off the icing, as this discolours if kept, and the marzipan, as this contains almond oil which turns rancid when stored. If it is likely that the cake will be used within the next year to 18 months, wrap it in plenty of acid-free tissue paper and store it in a cardboard box where the air can circulate round it. Do not keep it in an airtight tin or plastic box. Store in the coolest possible room, out of direct light. If it is likely that the cake is going to be kept for more than 18 months, wrap it in foil then put it into a double freezer bag and store it in the deep freeze, where it will keep well for up to two years.

Chapter 16

Photographs and video

As photographs and/or a video will be a lasting reminder of your wedding day, it is well worth hiring a professional for the occasion. You could also ask one or two friends who are keen photographers to bring their cameras and take some extra shots – this way you will get some very personal and informal pictures as well. If you want to upload photographs on to a website or send them by email, or if you want to be able to edit photographs on your computer, you can use a digital camera (see page 137), scan prints into your computer or ask for them to be processed on to a CD.

Personal recommendation is the best way to find a reliable photographer/video maker, but the *Yellow Pages* will supply many names, and you will probably be able to find one or two in your local high street. Bridal magazines and websites (page 233) are another good source, both of names of photographers/video makers and of ideas for different photographic styles.

Visit more than one and ask to see photographs/videos from several previous weddings. Make sure you are shown photographs/videos taken by the person you are planning to book, and not a compilation taken by several people. You will need to book about six months ahead of the wedding, possibly longer.

Photographs

Decide what style of photography you would like:

- do you want very formal pictures?
- are you interested in having some very informal, candid shots?
- would you like some photographs to be posed in a more original and artistic way, perhaps at a venue away from the church and reception such as a local park or riverside? Make sure your photographer is experienced at this type of work.

Your budget will dictate the number of photographs you ask for. A standard package usually contains 20 prints, starting with the groom's and best man's arrival at the church and ending at the reception when the cake is cut. You can add to this basic package as much as you like and can afford. The reportage style of wedding photography is very popular, and the finished album will tell the full story of the day, starting with the bride preparing to leave home and ending with the couple leaving the reception, with a mixture of traditional and informal photographs in between. However, you could pay £1,000 or more for this style of presentation, in a high-quality leather album.

Tip

Some couples use a professional photographer for the ceremony only and put a disposable flash camera on each table at the reception and ask the guests to take photographs. One of the bridesmaids could collect all the cameras at the end of the day. Another idea, which takes a little more preparation but produces a wonderful informal souvenir, is to prepare album pages with mounts, then ask someone to take Polaroid shots of guests at each table, making sure everyone is included. The shots can then be mounted on the album pages, and guests asked to write a message underneath their picture.

Spend time talking to your photographer in advance of the day. You will need to consider the following points.

- **Does the photographer make you feel relaxed and do you think you can work happily with him or her on the day?** A good photographer must be helpful and unobtrusive but also needs to be able to manage people, persuade them to pose and make sure that the photography does not hold up the proceedings for too long.
- **How will the key shots be covered?** Are you in agreement with the photographer about the level of formality and the mixture of formal and informal photographs? Are there any special shots you want or any guest of whom you would like a close-up?

- **The photographer will need a timetable of the day and a list of the names of the most important guests who must be included**. You can also give a list of shots which you particularly want.

- Organising **group photographs** takes time, and your guests will not want to be kept waiting at the wedding venue for too long. One way of getting round this is to drop the traditional receiving line and have the group photographs taken at the reception venue while the guests are arriving and being given a drink. Tell the key people in advance that they will be wanted for group photographs at the start of the reception and make sure they know where to go when they arrive.

- **Check with your minister where and when photography is allowed in church**. Policies vary, and while some ministers are happy to have a few discreet photographs taken during the service – although not always of the marriage itself – others ask for no flash or stipulate a number of pictures allowed, and some will permit no photography in the church at all.

The photographer broke the rules

Marianna's vicar specified that only one picture could be taken during the signing of the register. However, her photographer chose to ignore this and slipped in several extra photographs, thus annoying the vicar and causing everyone to feel uncomfortable – a fact that inevitably showed up in the photographs. Tell your photographer what is allowed and make sure he or she knows that you are happy to go along with any rules laid down by the vicar.

Negotiating a package

Most estimates include an album containing a specified number of photographs. Some packages also include two smaller versions of the main album to be given to each of the sets of parents, and you can also select some photographs to be printed in a larger size for framing; these are charged for in addition to the basic package. Some photographers quote for the amount of time they spend at your wedding on the day and charge extra for prints; others charge for prints but not for their time, while some base the cost on their time and offer unlimited prints.

Check for hidden extras such as development, VAT and delivery of proofs. If you want any special effects such as hand-tinting, sepia or black-and-white photographs, specify these when you make your booking and get confirmation of the cost. The photographer should send you a proof set of all the photographs taken, about a week after the wedding, and you can choose the ones you would like included in your album. You can also circulate the proofs round any others who might like to buy prints.

Popular wedding-day photographs

The list below covers most of the usual wedding photographs, but you will probably not want to have all of them.

Before the ceremony

- Bride and bridesmaids at home, preparing for the ceremony
- Close-up of bride before wedding
- Bride and father before leaving home
- Guests arriving at wedding venue
- Groom and best man at wedding venue before the ceremony
- Ushers at the wedding venue
- Bridesmaids and bride's mother arriving at wedding venue
- Bride and father arriving at wedding venue

At a register office/approved venue

Check whether there are any restrictions on where you can have photographs taken inside the venue.

In the church (if permitted)

- Bride's procession down the aisle
- The marriage ceremony (if permitted)
- Exchange of rings
- Signing of the register
- Musicians performing
- Bride and groom walking back down the aisle
- Bride and groom emerging from church

After the ceremony

- Bride and groom together
- Couple with bridesmaids and/or pages
- Couple with best man, bridesmaids and/or pages
- Bridesmaids and pages
- Couple with bride's parents
- Couple with groom's parents
- Couple with both sets of parents
- Couple with all family members of both sides
- Couple with all friends
- Entire wedding party
- Guests throwing confetti
- Couple leaving for reception

At the reception

- Receiving line
- Informal photographs during reception
- Top table
- Each side table
- Speeches: bride's father, groom, best man
- Cutting the cake
- First dance (bride and groom)
- Bride throwing bouquet
- Couple leaving reception

Other shots

- Portrait of bride
- Portrait of groom
- Close-up of ring(s) on finger
- Other special requests

Insurance

Ensure that your photographer is covered by a professional indemnity, which covers camera problems and lost or damaged film. Insurance cannot cover points of style, so if the photographs are not what you wanted or hoped for you will have to seek compensation from the photographer directly. If you take out wedding insurance (see Chapter 21), most policies cover you for the cost of a retake if the photographer does not show up on the day or the films or negatives are lost or damaged.

Photography checklist

Name of photographer	
Address	
Telephone/fax/email	
Contact	
Date booked	
Confirmed in writing	
Agreed fee	
What is included in the package?	
Time of photographer's arrival at bride's home/wedding venue	
Time of photographer's departure from the reception	
Date proofs will be supplied	
Special effects requested	

Digital photography

Digital cameras are very popular and can produce pictures of a quality comparable to those taken with film cameras, that you can share without the cost of endless reprints.

- Digital cameras do not use film, but store images digitally which can be downloaded on to a computer, then sent to others via email, or burnt on to a CD or DVD. Most film processors will put your digital photos on to CD for you, and make prints if you want them. You'll only save on processing costs if you don't want any prints at all, as printing them yourself also takes time and money, since you'll need to use high-quality glossy paper and a good colour printer.

137

- You can view each image before you decide which to print. You can crop, enhance and size pictures, and insert them into documents or web pages, or send them as emails.
- Most digital cameras come with software to edit the pictures, or you could use a specialised package like PhotoShop Elements or Paint Shop Pro.
- As well as the cost of the camera itself, you'll also need an up-to-date computer, appropriate software and a colour printer, making this an expensive option if you don't already own these items. However, using a digital camera, or even a film one and scanning the prints, is far cheaper than using a professional photographer, and you will own all the photos and can make as many copies as you want.

Things to consider

A camera's resolution determines the level of detail (although not necessarily the quality) it will be able to reproduce in its images. This directly affects the size of the prints you can make without the images becoming pixellated. Some 2-megapixel cameras cost under £100 and can produce reasonable 6x4 prints. If you are buying only to put pictures on your website or email them to friends, you can get away with a cheaper camera because the resolution of your PC monitor will be the limiting factor, and you won't achieve any better results with a more costly camera.

If this is your sole source of wedding photos, you'd be wise to opt for a camera with a higher spec. You can buy 4–5-megapixel cameras with a small zoom for under £300, while a top-end 6–8-megapixel camera with a big zoom costs between £500 and £800.

Video

More and more people are having professional videos made of their wedding day. It is tempting to ask a friend who owns a camcorder or is willing to hire one to do this for you, and you will certainly make a big saving. However, producing a well-shot, watchable video takes some skill, and you need to be certain that your friend is up to the task and is happy to concentrate on filming rather than entering into the fun of the occasion. Of course, if you are not worried about the occasional wobble or muffled sound, then an amateur video is worth considering. Digital camcorders give better results (see page 140).

If you decide to hire a professional, you should follow the same selection procedure as for a photographer. Styles of video vary, so look at a few samples to find the type that best suits you. Any reputable video service will provide insurance, and some also offer a customer dissatisfaction clause. With this, financial compensation may be available if an independent arbitration panel judges the final product to be of an inferior standard to that agreed in your contract.

Tips for making an amateur video

- Well in advance, draw up a list of shots that should definitely be included. You can shadow the official photographer and take some film from the sidelines as the main shots are set up – but do not get in the way.
- Remember to take a spare battery and plenty of videotape.
- Visit the church and reception venue ahead of the day if possible and work out the best positions for your shots. Check the position of useful power sockets.
- If you use a separate microphone, which will give good sound quality during the ceremony and speeches, position it where guests are unlikely to brush against it or knock it over.
- Use a hand-held microphone and ask guests to speak directly to the camera.
- Take as many shots as you can of people smiling and laughing.
- You will get a much better finished result if you can edit the film, so that shots can be shortened or intercut.
- Use shots of the church/wedding venue interior, or close-ups of floral arrangements or the bridal bouquet, to intersperse with the action shots.
- Be on the lookout for unusual or amusing shots.
- Keep the camera steady, using a tripod when necessary.
- Each sequence should be fairly short, otherwise the finished film will run for hours.
- Be sparing with your use of the zoom lens.
- Bookshops and libraries have a wide stock of books with detailed information on making a successful amateur video.

As with photography, you should be able to agree on a package deal, which will include a specified number of copies of the video and will stipulate at what stage the filming will start and finish. Check with your minister that he or she does not object to a video being made of the ceremony. (You will probably have to pay the church a small fee for having a video of the ceremony.) Remember that to achieve the best effects the video company may have to set up microphones and extra lighting.

Digital camcorders

Using a digital rather than an analogue camcorder does away with problems of poor resolution and grainy pictures, but you will need to pay a minimum of £300 for a digital camcorder and many models cost much more. Using your own camcorder, rather than hiring a professional, means you own copyright and can make as many copies as you like. The recording can be played back on your television, but not on a VHS video recorder.

The process of editing footage from a digital or analogue camcorder and burning it to disc so that you can share your video with friends and family is fairly straightforward:

- You will need: video-capture card for your computer, DVD burner, a high-spec computer.
- Step one: plug your camcorder into your computer and transfer its footage so you'll be able to edit it.
- Step two: edit your footage using the editing software that came with your DVD burner or a stand-alone package. Be sure to divide your footage into scenes or chapters so you'll be able to skip straight to the ceremony, for instance.
- Step three: 'render' the footage – this compresses the video so it will fit on a DVD, and formats it. It can take a while, so you might want to leave it to run overnight.
- Step four: burn the file to disc. Be sure to burn in a write-once format like DVD-/+R so it'll play on a wide range of DVD players.

Video checklist

Name of video company	
Address	
Telephone/fax/email	
Contact	
Date booked	
Confirmed in writing	
Agreed fee	
What is included in the package?	
Time of video maker's arrival at bride's home/wedding venue	
Time of video maker's departure from the reception	
When will the video be delivered?	

Chapter 17

Civil ceremonies

For many years the proportion of civil to religious marriages was roughly equal, but since the introduction of the 1994 law permitting non-religious weddings to take place at premises other than register offices, the number of civil marriages has been steadily increasing, until currently nearly two-thirds of all weddings are civil. Many of these ceremonies take place at register offices, but in 2002 over one-third of couples were married in alternative licensed premises, and this number continues to rise as more and more venues are licensed, and the choice increases. For more information about approved premises see Chapter 2, page 19.

Whether you choose to hold your civil ceremony in a register office or elsewhere, you will have to satisfy various legal criteria before you can marry (see Appendix).

The wedding day

The arrangements and timings for a civil wedding will vary considerably, depending on whether you have chosen to have a very quiet register office ceremony, a grand-scale wedding at approved premises, or something in between. The two case histories on pages 145–150, give some idea of what is involved at either end of the spectrum.

You can arrive at the wedding venue together or separately. Remember that register offices allow a fairly brief period for each wedding, so time your arrival for about ten minutes before the ceremony is due to begin. At approved premises the reception is sometimes held at the same venue as the ceremony, so there is unlikely to be more than one wedding on the same day. You can have a best man and bridesmaids if you wish, but all that the law requires is two adult witnesses.

Before the register office ceremony, you and your guests will gather in an ante-room. Wherever the marriage takes place, the couple have a brief private interview with the superintendent registrar before the ceremony, in which all details are checked for accuracy and the attendance fee is collected. The couple and guests then assemble in the room where the marriage is to be held.

The civil ceremony

When the law changes in 2005/6, the exact words used in the civil ceremony will no longer be prescribed. At the moment, certain parts of the ceremony are obligatory, but in places you can choose from a variety of wordings, as indicated below. At most register offices the superintendent registrar offers a choice of additional wordings to embellish the ceremony printed below, and you can incorporate these as you wish. You may also be able to add some words of your own.

The ceremony begins with the superintendent registrar saying: *'This place in which you are now met has been duly sanctioned according to the law for the celebration of marriages. You are here to witness the joining in matrimony of (man's full name) and (woman's full name). If any person present knows of any lawful impediment to this marriage, he should declare it now.'*

The superintendent registrar asks the couple to stand. The guests remain seated. The superintendent registrar confirms the couple's full names and then says to them: *'Before you are joined in matrimony I have to remind you of the solemn and binding character of the ceremony of marriage. Marriage according to the law of this country is the union of one man with one woman, voluntarily entered into for life, to the exclusion of all others. Now I am going to ask each of you in turn to declare that you do not know of any lawful reason why you should not be married to each other.'*

The couple in turn then repeat, either: *'I do solemnly declare that I know not of any lawful impediment why I, (full name), may not be joined in matrimony to (full name).'*
or
'I declare that I know of no legal reason why I, (full name), should not be joined in marriage to (full name).'
or
In response to the question: *'Are you, (full name), free lawfully to marry (full name)?'* respond, *'I am'*.

The superintendent registrar then says to all those present: *'Now the solemn moment has come for these two persons to contract the marriage before you, their witnesses. Will you all please stand.'*

In turn, the man and then the woman take their partner by the hand and repeat either: *'I call upon these persons here present to witness that I, (full name), do take thee, (full name), to be my lawful wedded wife/husband.'*

or

'I (full name) take you (or thee) (full name) to be my wedded wife/husband.'

There is no legal obligation to give or exchange a wedding ring or rings. If you do use rings, you will be asked to take the ring and place it on the other's ring finger and hold it there. At this point you may be allowed to personalise your vows if you wish. Alternatively, the superintendent registrar may be able to suggest different forms of words, such as: *'I give/accept this ring as a token of our marriage.'*

or

'Receive this ring as a token of my love and our marriage, a symbol of all that we have promised and all that we now share.'

Then the superintendent registrar says: *'(Full name) and (full name), you have both made the declarations prescribed by law, and have made a solemn and binding contract with each other, in the presence of the witnesses here assembled. You are now husband and wife together.'*

After a pause, where the couple may kiss each other and be congratulated by the guests, the superintendent registrar says: *'Will you now all please be seated while the register is signed.'*

The register is signed by the couple, two witnesses, the registrar and the superintendent registrar. A copy is written on to a marriage certificate which is given to the couple.

Leaving the civil ceremony

At approved premises you will probably be having the reception at the same venue, and will have already discussed where to take photographs.

For a register office wedding, you should be able to spend some time outside taking photographs, although depending on where the office is sited you may prefer to have them taken elsewhere. On a busy day the next wedding party will be arriving soon after your ceremony is over, so bear this in mind when briefing a photographer.

In either setting, find out what the policy is on confetti.

Personalising a civil ceremony

In addition to the words printed above – which must be included by law – you may be able to add personal touches to a civil ceremony in the form of non-religious music, poetry, readings or vows (see Chapter 14). However, you must discuss any additions with the superintendent registrar when booking the wedding. Some will allow only minor inclusions, regardless of whether you are marrying in a register office or approved premises, while others are happy to allow you more freedom. Whatever you want to add, *the content must be strictly non-religious*, and you should check first with the superintendent registrar that any material you want to use is permissible.

At approved premises, which are often booked for the ceremony and reception, thus allowing you more time, you may be able to organise a longer, more formal ceremony, possibly including a processional and recessional and the inclusion of more music. Check before making any arrangements, as some approved premises prefer to keep the ceremony brief and simple.

Case history

A small wedding at a register office

Kate and Rod wanted a wedding that was special, but with minimal fuss and low expense. Organisation went on over five months, and the ceremony was held at the local register office, followed by lunch at a hotel. Three months later the couple held a party for a wider group of friends.

Guests and gifts

Rod designed and produced the invitations on his computer. Twenty-five guests, including one child (whose mum brought his lunch with her), came to the ceremony and lunch. As wedding presents, Kate and Rod asked for gift vouchers from two specified shops. Eighty people came to the party, and the invitations made it clear that this was a 'don't-bring-a-present' event.

On the wedding day

Guests parked at the hotel where the reception was to be held, and walked to the nearby register office. Kate, who wore a pale blue suit and navy hat and carried a bouquet, arrived first with her family, while Rod, who hired a black lounge suit, came along later.

The ceremony

The couple had made a tape of two French waltzes, a stately one, which was played as everyone entered, and a more lively tune, composed and recorded by friends, which was played during the signing of the register. Two poems were read by guests, *The Confirmation* by Edwin Muir after the initial vows, and *The Frog Prince* by Stevie Smith at the end. The registrar checked both poems before the ceremony to ensure that they had no religious content and were not flippant.

Photography

A professional photographer took just 12 shots, some at the register office and some at the hotel where the lunch was held.

The reception

After drinking sparkling wine provided by the hotel, chatting, and having formal and informal photographs taken in the hotel gardens, the wedding party sat down to a three-course lunch. Kate and Rod provided their own wine to go with the meal, and the hotel charged £5 per bottle corkage. Tables were decorated with small posies. There were no formal speeches, just a couple of toasts with champagne, again provided by the hotel. The single-tier fruit cake was bought from a local shop and iced professionally in a simple design.

After lunch, the wedding party went to Kate and Rod's house, where friends helped by serving tea and, later, by driving the couple the 30 miles to a B&B on the coast, where they had a three-night stay. The couple took their main honeymoon, in Crete, three months later, immediately after the party.

The party

Three months after the wedding, Kate and Rod held a party to which they invited family and a wide circle of friends. A friend arranged the hire of a hall at a discount and a buffet was supplied by a local caterer, although the couple overestimated and ordered too much food. The couple provided a small amount of drink, asked friends to bring a bottle, and also had a pay-bar, although hardly any of the guests made use of this. A band played ceilidh music and there was a toast, speeches and another cake.

Timings
On the wedding day:

11.00	Leave home, drive to hotel and park car. Walk to register office, arrive 11.15.
11.30	Wedding ceremony and photographs.
12.10	Walk back to hotel for reception.
12.30–1.45	Wine, chat and photographs.
1.45	Lunch.
4.00	Leave hotel with guests and go home for tea.
8.00	Driven to honeymoon B&B.

What it cost
The wedding day

Ceremony and certificate	£97.50
Kate's outfit	£340.00
Hire of Rod's outfit	£50.00
Bouquet/buttonhole	£78.50
Photographer: 12 shots, plus album	£150.00
Reception: hotel bill (including lunch for 26, drinks, corkage and VAT)	£821.00
Cake	£50.00
Wine	£150.00
Total	£1,737.00

The party

Hire of hall and cash bar (with discount via friend)	£50.00
Band	£250.00
Buffet	£500.00
Spanish sparkling wine for toasts	£60.00
Cake	£56.00
Total (not including honeymoon)	£916.00

Case history

A family wedding at approved licensed premises

Chloe and Monty spent ten months planning their wedding. The organisation was very time-consuming, as both were living and working in London, but the wedding was taking place near their home town, about 80 miles away, and they made numerous trips to order flowers, buy the dress, fix the reception details and so on.

Both ceremony and reception were held in the Council Chamber of the Town Hall, a large room beautifully decorated with pictures and velvet hangings.

Guests and gifts

Invitations were ordered from a department store. There were 88 guests, including seven children. The couple asked for gift vouchers, and were also given money and other presents.

On the day

Chloe arrived in a gold Jaguar, belonging to and driven by a friend. She wore a classic ivory satin wedding dress and tiara, and was attended by two bridesmaids and a page, who wore outfits from chain-store wedding collections. Bride and bridesmaids carried posies, and buttonholes were provided for all the guests. Monty hired a blue velvet Mozart-style jacket and navy trousers, plus a gold brocade waistcoat and cravat.

The ceremony

The live music was provided mainly by friends and family. A brass quartet played the 'Minuet' from Handel's *Water Music* at the entrance of the bride and 'La Rejouissance' from Handel's *Music for the Royal Fireworks* for the recession. The groom's brother, accompanied by a hired harpist, sang three traditional folk songs during the ceremony, *The Lark in the Clear Air*, *I will Give my Love an Apple* and *My Love's an Arbutus*. The groom's sister read a poem, *I Will Be Here* by Steven Curtis Chapman, and his grandmother read a Celtic blessing, *May Peace Guard the Door of Your House*. The bride's father gave her away. The couple wrote their own vows.

Photography

A professional photographer took over 200 shots before and after the ceremony, from which the couple chose 30 to make up an album. The bride's brother took video film of the whole day. Taking the photographs took longer than anticipated, which had a knock-on effect on timings for the rest of the day, but fortunately the venue was flexible and allowed the wedding party to continue for an extra half-hour, until 11.30pm.

The reception

Once the photography was over, guests were served buck's fizz and had a chance to sit down and chat. The couple had intended to have a receiving line, but abandoned the idea, because everyone had already had a chance to meet and time was running short. A sit-down three-course meal, provided by caterers and served by waitresses followed, accompanied by wines bought by the couple. The caterers did not charge corkage. One of the catering team acted as informal master of ceremonies, and introduced the speeches, toasts and the cutting of the cake. After the meal a four-piece folk band plus caller played for a barn dance which ended at 11.30pm. During this time a pay-bar was available, and in the middle of the evening bread, cheese, pâté and soft drinks were served. The couple stayed the night at a local hotel, and left next morning for a ten-day honeymoon in Italy.

Timings

On the day:

2.30	Bride arrives, sees registrar.
2.40–3.00	Ceremony with music.
3.15–4.30	Photographs.
4.30–5.30	Buck's fizz, sit down and chat.
5.30	Wedding breakfast served.
8.00	Meal ends, band set up.
9.30	Light refreshments served.
8.30–11.30	Barn dance.

What it cost

Hire of venue, ceremony and certificate	£1,529.00
Chloe's outfit	£500.00
Make-up lesson and make-up	£150.00

Hairdresser	£60.00
Hire of Monty's outfit	£220.00
Attendants' outfits	£250.00
Flowers	£420.00
Hire of harpist and trombonist	£180.00
Photographer: 30 shots plus album	£425.00
Reception food: sit-down meal, plus evening refreshments	£1,750.00
Drinks: wine, champagne and soft drinks, all bought by the couple	£385.00
Cake	£130.00
Band	£400.00
Thank-you gifts	£200.00
Insurance	£60.00
Stationery	£110.00
Total (not including honeymoon)	£6,769.00

Alternative ceremonies

Although not legally binding, an alternative ceremony can make a good follow-on from a simple civil marriage and enables you to have exactly the sort of ceremony you would like. You could create your own ceremony and write your own vows, which need not follow a particular set of beliefs but which can, if you wish, include religious elements. See the books mentioned on page 232 for different types of alternative ceremony.

A humanist ceremony

Humanists do not believe in any god, an afterlife or the supernatural. Their beliefs are founded on the idea that people should try to live full and happy lives and, in doing this, make it easier for other people to do the same. A humanist wedding ceremony embodies these ideas and can be tailored to fit your wishes and personalities. You can choose from a wide selection of poetry and readings, and whichever type of music you like to enhance the proceedings. Contact the British Humanist Association★ for more details.

If you are considering having a humanist ceremony it is a good idea to explain in advance to your guests, perhaps in a note sent out

Suresh and Ruth

Suresh, who is Indian, and Ruth, who is English, had differing views from their parents regarding their wedding ceremony. Their parents felt that the religious element was important, although this would create difficulties because of the difference in cultures and expectations. Suresh and Ruth wanted a non-religious event. So they chose to have a humanist ceremony, which they wrote themselves, straight after their civil marriage. They wanted a ceremony where they could have control over the words they used and the content. The humanist ceremony accorded with their belief that people should have freedom of choice in the main decisions of life, and should be able to celebrate one of the principal milestones of their lives in a non-religious way. The ceremony gave them the opportunity to make a serious public commitment to share their lives, despite the cultural and racial differences in their backgrounds, in a setting that both found poignant, moving and very pertinent to each of them as individuals and as a couple.

A humanist celebrant, with whom they had met beforehand to discuss the content of the ceremony, conducted it for them. In his introduction, the celebrant said: '*Ruth and Suresh recognise the uniqueness of their marriage, which crosses cultural and racial boundaries. It is very important to them that everyone, whatever his or her beliefs, feels comfortable about the proceedings and respects the decisions they have made. Above all they want friends and relatives to be a part of their day and witness their commitment to each other.*'

Brothers of the bride and groom each gave a reading, then the couple repeated marriage vows similar to those used in a church service but without any mention of God. They exchanged rings, and music was played while they signed a register. The proceedings concluded with the bride's sister reading from an American Indian ceremony: '*Now you will feel no rain, for each of you will be shelter for the other. Now you will feel no cold, for each of you will be warmth to the other. Now there is no more loneliness. Now you are two persons, but there is only one life before you. Go now to your dwelling to enter into the days of your life together. And may your days be good and long upon the earth.*'

with the invitations, exactly who humanists are and what they believe. You should also remember that such a ceremony may not be entirely acceptable to others, such as your parents, particularly if they would prefer you to have a ceremony that meets their own religious beliefs.

Chapter 18

Religious ceremonies

Most religious ceremonies follow a set traditional procedure, which you can discuss with the minister when you make the initial arrangements. You will have to satisfy various legal criteria before you will be permitted to have any sort of religious ceremony (see the Appendix).

Church of England marriage ceremony

When you first visit the minister who will conduct your marriage he or she will tell you about the procedure for arranging the wedding, publishing the banns and organising the ceremony itself. Details of the documents you need to produce at this meeting are given on page 217. At this first meeting you can set the date and time of the wedding and discuss details such as who will play the organ, whether you want to use the church choir, your choice of music and where you can put flowers. You can also book a date and time for a rehearsal if your wedding is not too far in the future.

The minister will want to discuss the religious significance of the marriage service with you, so you may be asked to attend a series of marriage preparation sessions, during which the ceremony will be explained in detail and you will have the opportunity to think through the implications of marriage. The ceremonies of the Church of Scotland*, Church in Wales and Church of Ireland are very similar to that of the Church of England. See pages 30–31 for details of the Church of England ceremony of blessing for second marriages.

Catherine and Alistair

Catherine and Alistair got married by special licence (see page 222) because neither of them lived in the parish of the church in which they were planning to marry. 'The vicar gave us the impression that he would arrange the licence but he went on holiday without having done so, and the deaconess who took over assumed that we had made the arrangements ourselves. Five days before the wedding we realised that we didn't have the licence, and my fiancé had to visit Lambeth Palace to sort it out. It was a close-run thing, and a better discussion, with proper clarification over who was responsible for what, would have avoided it.'

Order of service

You will need to discuss the order of the service and which version of the ceremony you would like to use (see below). The service usually begins with a few words of introduction and a hymn, followed by the marriage itself. After the marriage has taken place there may be prayers, further hymns and possibly an address and some readings before the register is signed. For more information on choosing music and readings, see Chapter 14. Once you have worked out the exact order and decided on the music and readings, you can draw up an order of service for printing (see page 125).

Versions of the marriage service

There are three current versions of the marriage service to choose from. The versions dating from 1966 and 2000 are available as inexpensive booklets from Church House Bookshop at the General Synod of the Church of England★, so it is possible to study them in detail before deciding which version you would like to use.

- The version from the **1662 Book of Common Prayer** – The language is old-fashioned, and the bride's promise to obey her husband is an obligatory part of the service. It is not used very frequently but it is sometimes chosen by couples who like the older, more formal language and want a very traditional ceremony.

- **The form of Solemnisation of Matrimony 1966** – The language is similar in style to that of the 1662 version, but the bride's promise to obey and serve her husband is optional, and the language of the introduction is more moderate.
- **The 2000 Marriage Service (Common Worship)** — The language is modern and direct. Again, the bride can choose whether or not she wants to promise to obey, and the couple can decide whether or not they want the possible future birth of children to be mentioned.

When the law changes in 2005/6, the exact form of words used to contract the marriage will no longer be prescribed by law. It is not yet clear how this will affect the wording of the marriage ceremony. In the details given below, wordings are given from the 1966 and 2000 versions for comparison.

The ceremony

- See page 62 for timings leading up to the ceremony on the day. Before the service starts the organist plays gentle music to create the right mood in the church. When the bride arrives the organist plays the music for the processional, and the groom and best man stand and move to the head of the aisle. The congregation then rises.
- The bride holds her father's right arm and, followed by the bridesmaids and pages, walks slowly down the aisle. The chief bridesmaid walks directly behind the bride, followed by the other attendants.
- The groom and best man may turn to greet the bride as she walks down the aisle or at the chancel steps.
- At the chancel steps the bride lifts back her veil if she is wearing one, perhaps helped by the chief bridesmaid. She hands her bouquet to the chief bridesmaid, who keeps it until the register has been signed.

The marriage

The minister greets the bridal party and congregation with a few introductory words and then begins the ceremony, which lasts about half an hour, depending on how many hymns and readings you are adding (with three hymns, two readings and an address, the service will take about 50 minutes). The congregation remain standing for the marriage itself and the hymns but may sit for the address and sit or kneel during the prayers. These moves can either be included in an order of service sheet, or the minister will tell the congregation what to do.

The service begins with a few words on the significance of marriage and its purposes:

1966: *'Dearly beloved, we are gathered here in the sight of God and in the face of this congregation, to join together this man and this woman in Holy Matrimony; which is an honourable estate, instituted of God himself, signifying unto us the mystical union that is betwixt Christ and his Church . . .'*

2000: *'In the presence of God, Father, Son and Holy Spirit, we have come together to witness the marriage of N. (groom) and N. (bride), to pray for God's blessing on them, to share their joy and to celebrate their love. Marriage is a gift of God in creation through which husband and wife may know the grace of God. It is given that as man and woman grow together in love and trust, they shall be united with one another in heart, body and mind, as Christ is united with his bride, the Church. The gift of marriage brings husband and wife together in the delight and tenderness of sexual union and joyful commitment to the end of their lives. It is given as the foundation of family life in which children are [born and] nurtured and in which each member of the family, in good times and bad, may find strength, companionship and comfort, and grow to maturity in love . . .'*

The minister then asks whether any member of the congregation knows of any reason why the couple should not be married:

1966: *'Therefore if any man can shew any just cause, why they may not lawfully be joined together, let him now speak, or else hereafter for ever hold his peace.'*

2000: *'First, I am required to ask anyone present who knows a reason why these persons may not lawfully marry, to declare it now.'*

The minister then asks the couple if either knows of any reason why they should not marry.

1966: *'I require and charge you both, as ye will answer at the dreadful day of judgement when the secrets of all hearts be disclosed, that if either of you know any impediment, why ye may not be lawfully joined together in Matrimony, ye do confess it. For be ye well assured, that so many as are coupled together otherwise than God's word doth allow are not joined together by God; neither is their Matrimony lawful.'*

2000: *'The vows you are about to take are to be made in the presence of God, who is judge of all and who knows all the secrets of our hearts; therefore if either of you knows a reason why you may not lawfully marry, you must declare it now.'*

The couple are then asked in turn if each will marry the other:

1966: *'N. Wilt thou have this woman to thy wedded wife, to live together according to God's law in the holy estate of Matrimony? Wilt thou love her, comfort her, honour and keep her, in sickness and in health? And, forsaking all other, keep thee only unto her, so long as ye both shall live?'*

2000: *'N., will you take N. to be your husband? Will you love him, comfort him, honour and protect him, and, forsaking all others, be faithful to him as long as you both shall live?'*

The bride and groom respond, *'I will.'*

1966: The minister asks who gives the woman to be married. The bride's father takes the bride's right hand and gives it to the minister who places it in the groom's right hand. This concludes the bride's father's role in the ceremony, and he steps back and joins the bride's mother in the front pew. Some couples prefer to omit this part of the ceremony.

2000: After the bride has responded, *'I will'*, the minister says to the congregation, *'Will you, the families and friends of N. and N., support and uphold them in their marriage now and in the years to come?'* The congregation responds: *'We will.'*

In this ceremony, the giving away of the bride by her father is also optional, but may be performed at this stage, as in the 1966 version. Alternatively, the minister may say to the parents of both bride and groom: *'N. and N. have declared their intention towards each other. As their parents, will you now entrust your son and daughter to one another as they come to be married?'* The parents respond, *'We will.'*

Next the couple make their wedding vows, taking it in turn to repeat the words after the minister:

1966: *'I N. take thee N. to my wedded wife, to have and to hold from this day forward, for better, for worse; for richer, for poorer; in sickness and in health; to love and to cherish till death us do part, according to God's holy law; and thereto I give thee my troth.'* (Women have the option to obey in this service.)

2000: *'I, N., take you, N., to be my husband, to have and to hold from this day forward; for better, for worse, for richer, for poorer, in sickness and in health, to love and to cherish (or, to love, cherish, and obey), till death us do part, according to God's holy law. In the presence of God I make this vow.'*

Some couples learn their vows off by heart so they can say them to each other without needing to be prompted by the minister.

The best man places the ring(s) on an open prayer book, which the minister offers him. The rings are blessed, then the minister gives the bride's ring to the groom, who places it on her finger and repeats the words:

1966: *'With this ring I thee wed; with my body I thee honour; and all my worldly goods with thee I share: In the name of the Father, and of the Son, and of the Holy Ghost. Amen.'*

2000: *'I give you this ring as a sign of our marriage. With my body I honour you, all that I am I give to you, and all that I have I share with you, within the love of God, Father, Son, and Holy Spirit.'*

If rings are exchanged these words are also repeated by the bride as she places a ring on the groom's finger. The minister then pronounces the couple husband and wife:

1966: *'Those whom God hath joined together let no man put asunder . . . I pronounce that they be man and wife together, In the name of the Father, and of the Son, and of the Holy Ghost. Amen.'*

2000: *'I therefore proclaim that they are husband and wife. Those whom God has joined together let no one put asunder.'*

The ceremony continues with prayers, hymns, readings and/or an address. If the service includes communion or mass it will take place at this point. The service ends with the signing of the register.

Signing the register

The bride and groom, chief bridesmaid and best man, other attendants, bride's and groom's parents and minister are all present at the signing of the register. This can either take place in the vestry (in which case the bridal party gain a few minutes of privacy in which they can relax a little before leaving church) or at a side table, in view of the congregation. Music is usually played or sung while the congregation wait for the register to be signed.

The marriage register is signed by the minister, the bride, using her unmarried name, the groom and two adult witnesses – perhaps the two fathers or the two mothers or the best man and chief bridesmaid. Decide before the ceremony who will sign. The marriage certificate, which is a copy of the register entry, is given to the couple by the minister (although the best man will usually take charge of it during the day).

Seating plan during the marriage

	ALTAR		
	Minister		
Bride's father	BRIDE	GROOM	Best Man
	Chief Bridesmaid		
	Attendants		
Bride's mother		Groom's parents	
Bride's close family		Groom's close family	
Other members of bride's family		Other members of groom's family	
Friends		Friends	

After the register has been signed, the bridal party and congregation leave the church. The chief bridesmaid returns the bride's bouquet to her and arranges her train. The bride takes her husband's left arm, the organist begins the recessional music and the bridal party leaves the church in the following order: bride and groom, chief bridesmaid and best man, other attendants, bride's mother with groom's father, and groom's mother with bride's father. The congregation follow, with those seated at the front of the church leaving before those seated at the back.

Outside the church

Once outside the church, photographs are taken.

- The congregation may shower the couple with confetti if allowed by the minister. Alternatives to confetti are rice, which can sting but may be cleared up for you by the birds, or flower petals which could be provided in baskets by bridesmaids.

- The best man helps the photographer to marshal the guests into groups for the photographs.
- The best man or ushers should check inside the church to make sure that nothing has been left behind, including top hats and gloves belonging to the bridal party, cameras and umbrellas.
- When the photographs have all been taken, the bride and groom leave the church for the reception. Next to leave are the couple's parents and the bridesmaids and pages. Guests follow on, and it is up to the best man to make sure that everyone has the means to get to the reception. He should be last to leave the church but must also try not to arrive too late at the reception, where he may be wanted to take part in the receiving line.

Roman Catholic ceremony

The Roman Catholic ceremony can be conducted with or without a nuptial mass (a wedding without nuptial mass is usually celebrated when one partner is non-Christian). The minister is normally a priest, but if the ceremony is without a mass, he may be a deacon. The ceremony is similar to that of the Church of England and begins with a welcome, an introduction, and Bible readings but has a responsorial psalm. After the minister's address comes the marriage rite:

The minister then says: *'You have come together in this church so that the Lord may seal and strengthen your love in the presence of the Church's minister and this community. Christ abundantly blesses this love. He has already consecrated you in baptism and now he enriches and strengthens you by a special sacrament so that you may assume the duties of marriage in mutual and lasting fidelity. And so, in the presence of this Church, I ask you to state your intentions.*

'I shall now ask you if you freely undertake the obligations of marriage, and to state that there is no legal impediment to your marriage.'

He then asks the couple three questions to which they respond in turn after each question *'I am'*:

'Are you ready freely and without reservation to give yourselves to each other in marriage?'

'Are you ready to love and honour each other as man and wife for the rest of your lives?'

'Are you ready to accept children lovingly from God, and bring them up according to the law of Christ and his Church?'

Finally, the couple take their vows with words similar to those in the Church of England ceremony. The bride does not promise to obey.

Minister: 'You have declared your consent before the Church. May the Lord in his goodness strengthen your consent and fill you both with his blessings. What God has joined together, let no man put asunder.'

The rings are then blessed and given with the words:

'May the Lord bless this ring (these rings) which you give (to each other) as the sign of your love and fidelity.'

The couple in turn then say:

'N. (Christian name only) take this ring as a sign of my love and fidelity. In the name of the Father, and of the Son, and of the Holy Spirit.'

If the marriage ceremony is taking place within a mass, the mass continues after the exchange of rings. A nuptial blessing is given by the minister before communion in a nuptial mass, or after the intercessions in a ceremony without mass. The signing of the register follows the final prayers and hymn, and the couple then leave church together.

Non-conformist or free church ceremonies

Marriages which take place in churches such as Methodist, Baptist and United Reformed Church use a ceremony very similar to that of the Church of England. The order of service may be slightly altered.

Quaker ceremony

Marriages take place in a specially appointed 'meeting for worship' which mainly follows the usual simple Quaker practice of prayerful silence, with an opportunity for those present to offer their own blessings and good wishes. Local Quakers would hope to offer ongoing support to any couple 'married in the care of the meeting', and therefore expect a couple to have some involvement in the Quaker community, with one probably in membership, or strongly in sympathy with Quaker principles. Ample time should therefore be allowed for consulting the registering officer.

An explanation of the procedure is given, the couple then stand and make their declaration of marriage using these words: *'Friends, I take this my friend, (full name), to be my husband/wife, promising, through Divine assistance (or, with God's help), to be unto him/her a loving and faithful wife/husband, so long as we both on earth shall live.'*

Wedding rings are not formally exchanged during a Quaker wedding, but the couple may like to give each other a ring after making their declarations. They sign the Quaker marriage certificate in front of the first two witnesses and the certificate is read aloud by the registering officer, either immediately or towards the end of the meeting.

A period of silence then follows during which anyone present may speak, perhaps to pray, or offer their loving support. At the end of the meeting the couple and the registering officer sign the civil register; afterwards all those present sign the Quaker marriage certificate, as witnesses also.

Jewish ceremony

The wedding usually takes place in a synagogue, but other venues such as halls or hotel suites are also acceptable. A quorum or *minyan* of at least ten adult males for an orthodox service, or ten adult men and women for a non-orthodox service, should be present. Prior to the ceremony, the groom approaches the bride and lowers her veil over her face. Who accompanies the groom and bride to the flower-decorated wedding canopy or *chuppah* varies according to custom. Sometimes the groom may be escorted by his father and the bride's father, or by his parents; while the bride is escorted by the two mothers, or by her parents. Most often these days the bride is accompanied by her father to meet the groom. The bride can, if she so wishes, walk round the groom three or seven times, depending on custom, before standing on his right. While this is happening the rabbi or cantor chants a welcome blessing.

The ceremony itself begins with the rabbi reciting a blessing over a goblet of wine from which the bride and groom then drink. The groom places the wedding ring on the forefinger of the bride's right hand, saying *'Behold you are wedded to me with this ring according to the Law of Moses and Israel.'* (The bride may transfer the ring to her left hand after the ceremony.) The *ketubah* or marriage contract, which is written in Aramaic, has already been signed by the witnesses prior to the ceremony. The bride and groom do not have to sign the *ketubah* to make it valid in Jewish law, but may, if they wish, sign the abstract printed on the reverse side. The *ketubah* is read aloud, and the seven benedictions are recited or sung over a goblet of wine. Sometimes this is done by various guests. The bride and groom drink again from the goblet, and the groom then crushes a glass with his right foot.

The rabbi invokes the priestly blessing. The newly married couple then sign the civil contract of marriage (if they have not already had a civil wedding) and are then taken to a private room where they spend a short time together and break their fast, which commenced at dawn, before going on to the reception venue.

Hindu ceremony

Some Hindu weddings take place in halls adjoining temples, but more often than not venues such as civic suites and function rooms in hotels are used. The atmosphere at a Hindu wedding is colourful, noisy and fun, and many members of the couple's family, as well as their friends, are involved. The bride and groom sit under a canopy (*mandap*) or on a stage decorated with flowers, and a priest chants prayers and lights the sacred fire (*agni*). A Hindu wedding is valid only if the couple is married in front of a fire, said to be the eternal witness to the sacrament of marriage.

There are numerous variations to the wedding ceremony and its rituals, depending on the part of India, and even the individual community, from which the families come, and so the festivities could take up the best part of a day or even be spread over a couple of days. The single most important ritual, common to all Hindu ceremonies, is the *saptapadi*, the seven steps, or sometimes seven complete circuits, around the sacred fire taken by the bride and groom. The priest recites a series of *mantras* as the steps are taken, and asks Lord Vishnu to bless the bride and groom with food, strength, piety, children, wealth, comfort and health.

Another ritual observed at all Hindu weddings is the exchange of garlands of fragrant flowers between bride and groom as a symbol of their sharing the fragrance of life henceforth. Additionally, in most parts of India, especially the south, the tying of the *mangalsutra* is considered to be very important. A thread is knotted around the bride's neck: she will wear it (and a gold necklace, given at the same time), like a wedding ring, for the rest of her married life. (Hindu couples getting married in the West sometimes choose to have wedding rings.) A ritual that is essential in most north Indian weddings is the applying of *sindoor* (vermilion powder) to the parting of the bride's hair by the groom to indicate that she is married.

There are many other rituals, but none of these is by any means universal. *Mehendi*, the application of henna patterns to the bride's hands and feet, is a social occasion, which takes place a few days before the wedding, and is a women-only function, for family and close friends. During the wedding ceremony itself, in many parts of India the father gives the bride away (*kanya danam*), by reciting words from the epic story *Ramayana*, and pouring water on the couple's hands to symbolise the relinquishing of his parental authority. A very emotional custom, the *vidai* (departure), may take place at the end of the day-long ceremonies, as the bride's parents, close relatives and friends bid her farewell. Both bride and groom touch the feet of the elders as a mark of respect and to gain blessing for their new life.

Many families have social receptions in the evening; food, music and dancing all add to the sense of occasion.

Sikh ceremony

The Sikh culture has embraced some Hindu traditions and there are similarities between the wedding ceremonies of the two cultures. Like the Hindu ceremony, the Sikh ceremony takes place in the morning and celebrations can last the whole day. The wedding ceremony is a formal event usually held in the temple (*gudwara*). Inside the temple, guests must remove their shoes, wash their hands and cover their heads. In the prayer hall, the congregation sit on the floor facing the altar. After some prayers, the priest requests the bride's father to take one end of the brightly decorated long scarf (*laar*) which is draped round the groom's shoulders, and place it in the bride's hand. The other end is held by the groom. This signifies that the father is now giving his daughter away and that the couple are now partners who share one life. This is an emotional moment for the bride and her family. The couple hold the ends of the scarf throughout the ceremony.

The central part of the ceremony – *laama* — follows, when the groom leads the bride around the altar four times. Finally a hymn is sung to indicate that the couple are now married and the ceremony is over. Close relatives then take turns to bless the couple with garlands, sweetmeats and money. All the other guests then come up to the couple and offer gifts of money.

The departure (*dhol*) takes place at the end of the day and is a very emotional time for the bride's family and relatives. Each member wishes her good luck and bids her farewell as she leaves for her new home with the groom and his family. Today, especially in the West, the bride and groom may have already set up their own home, but it is still customary for them to spend the first few days after the wedding in the groom's family home so that the bride can get used to her new family. After that the couple may go on honeymoon.

Muslim ceremony

The wedding ceremony need not take place in a mosque, and any respected male may officiate. The bride is asked if she consents to the marriage. She may convey her consent through her guardian, usually her father, or she may answer herself. The groom is then asked if he accepts the marriage, with the agreed dowry that he will give to the bride.

These are the elements of the ceremony which are needed to meet Islamic requirements, but different cultures include extra traditions. After the wedding a celebration for the couple's families, friends and neighbours may be held days, or even weeks, later.

Chapter 19

Organising the reception

The reception accounts for a large percentage of the cost of the wedding. The exact amount depends on how long the reception lasts, the number of guests, the venue and the type of meal and entertainment. Ask yourselves:

- **how formal should the reception be**? This will affect your choice of venue, food and drink
- **how long will it last**? Shorter receptions are just as enjoyable as those that continue into the early hours of the morning, and leave both you and your guests less tired. This can be an important factor if you are setting off on a long journey to your honeymoon destination that day
- **what time of day will the reception begin**? The meal served will depend on the time of day you get married. Many people marry in the mid-afternoon so that they can serve an early evening meal followed by entertainment. However, you could have a late-morning ceremony followed by a lunch and leave during the afternoon
- **how many guests will be at the reception**? Some people have a fairly brief reception immediately after the wedding for a small number of close family and friends, then throw a big party for everyone else on their return from honeymoon, while others have a quiet ceremony but invite more people to come along to all, or part, of the reception.

Choosing a venue

Popular venues include hotels, restaurants, function rooms in pubs and sports clubs, village halls, marquees, your own or your parents' home. Allow plenty of time to shop around for a venue and compare

Juliet and Peter

Juliet and Peter had intended to fly off to the USA on the evening of their wedding day. 'In the end we had to change our plans because we couldn't get on the flight we wanted. I was very glad about this when it came to the day because although our reception, a sit-down lunch in a restaurant, ended at 5pm, I was feeling exhausted by then. Neither of us had slept well for the previous couple of nights with pre-wedding nerves, we'd both been up since 7am rushing around getting ready, and I'd hardly sat down during the reception because I was busy going round the tables talking to friends. We took a taxi from the reception to a good hotel, where we unwound over a light supper and spent the evening lazing about and talking over the day.'

costs carefully, as there can be huge variations between the prices of hiring the room, catering and wine. When you book a venue, confirm all the details in writing and leave nothing to chance. You can copy and complete the venue checklists given on pages 168–70, 172–4 and 176. The hotel checklist includes space for details of food, wine and entertainment, as these would be part of the total package. If you are using another type of venue, you will find separate checklists for food, drink and entertainment on pages 179, 182 and 198.

Before you settle on any restaurant or hotel, have a meal there so that you can judge whether the food is good, the facilities adequate and the atmosphere right.

Wherever you hold your reception, check the following:

- Is the room you would use large enough? Allow at least one square metre per person
- Are there enough toilets and sufficient cloakroom space?
- Are there plenty of parking spaces?
- Are there facilities for disabled guests or people who are elderly and frail? Some seating should be available even if the guests are to remain standing at the reception
- Is a separate room available where children could be entertained?
- How far is the reception venue from the place where the ceremony will be held? Try to keep the distance reasonably short.

Hotels

Most hotels can comfortably accommodate wedding parties of 50 to 100 guests, and some can cater for substantially more. At places where wedding receptions are held frequently, you should be able to arrange a package that includes all the catering, catering staff, wine and other drinks; the fee may also cover flowers, entertainment and a toastmaster. Check whether the venue can supply a cake stand and knife, a room where you can change into your going-away clothes, overnight accommodation for guests who need it and a safe place for displaying your wedding gifts.

The benefit of having your reception in a hotel is that you do not have to organise so much yourselves as the hotel will arrange the food, drink, entertainment and so on. Also, if you are having your civil wedding ceremony at a hotel, you will not have to travel anywhere to get to the reception. On the minus side, hotels can be expensive and rather impersonal, especially if a large number of receptions are held there; you may have to share some facilities if another reception is taking place on the same day; hotels often need to be booked many months in advance; and there may be restrictions on the amount of time you can spend there.

Hotel checklist

Name of hotel	
Address	
Telephone/fax/email	
Contact	
Date booking made	
Confirmed in writing	
Number of guests	
Time of arrival at venue	
Time of departure from venue	
Which rooms have been booked?	
Bar facilities	
Cloakroom/toilet facilities	

Any shared facilities?	
Heating requested	
Toastmaster booked	
Who will provide flowers?	
Where will flowers be put?	
Other decorations	
Where will gifts be displayed?	
Are they insured at the hotel?	
Where will bride and groom change?	
Is a room available for children?	

Food

Type of seating plan agreed on	
Which dishes will be served?	
Any special dietary requirements?	
Number of children's portions	
How many serving staff will be available?	
What time will the meal be served?	
Cost per head of food	

Drinks

	Type of drink	Quantity	Cost per bottle
On arrival			
With the meal			
After the meal			
Evening bar			
Corkage, if supplying own drinks			
Total cost of drink			£

(continued overleaf)

Entertainment		
Background music provided by		
From (time)	To (time)	Breaks
Cost	£	
Dance music provided by		
From (time)	To (time)	Breaks
Cost	£	
Children's entertainment provided by		
From (time)	To (time)	Breaks
Cost	£	

Summary of costs	
(a) Total cost of food	£
(b) Total cost of drink	£
(c) Total cost of entertainment	£
(d) Cost of hiring the venue	£
(e) Other items (make a detailed list)	£
(f)	£
(g)	£
(h)	£
(i)	£
(j)	£
(k) Service charge	£
Tips	£
VAT	£
TOTAL COST	£
Deposit paid	£
Balance due	£

Halls

If you have a smaller number of guests and a tight budget, consider hiring a hall or function room. Although rooms like these can be very well decorated and equipped, this is not always the case, so do pay a visit and check the facilities before making a booking. You will pay a fee for hiring the hall but will have to arrange catering and entertainment etc. yourself. Check:

- whether there are any rules about the consumption of alcohol and smoking on the premises
- that the hall can be heated adequately
- whether you need to hire crockery, glasses etc.
- what facilities exist for preparing and serving food: for example, how much refrigerator and worktop space is available; whether the facilities for clearing away and washing up are good; and, if you want hot food, whether there are enough ovens
- whether you will need to arrange for clearing away and washing up to be done
- that the seating is comfortable and there is enough of it
- whether there is a separate room where you can change
- that the venue's insurance covers loss of or damage to gifts
- how far ahead you need to book
- that someone can show you where everything is and how it works in advance
- how long before the event you can get access for decorating the hall and for caterers to set up.

Other hired venues

These include restaurants, or rooms in stately homes, castles, river boats, and so on. The number of possible venues to choose from is enormous, especially if you want to hold your reception some-where a bit different.

Points to remember are:

- your favourite restaurant may be able to offer superb food, but you need to check that it also has facilities for changing, parking and so on. You also need to make sure that the tables can be arranged so that, ideally, everyone can see the bride and groom. There may not be space for dancing or any sort of live entertainment

171

- if you book a sumptuous room in a historical building you may have to hire or order many extra items, such as food and drink, tables, chairs, cutlery and crockery, glasses, serving staff, ovens and refrigerators. Even if the fee for the room itself is reasonable, these extras can add dramatically to the overall cost, so work out your budget carefully before committing yourself
- you need to check any time restrictions. Restaurants, for instance, often ask wedding parties to leave by about 5pm so that they can clear the room and lay the tables for the evening.

Venue checklist

Name of venue	
Address	
Telephone/fax/email	
Contact	
Date booking made	
Confirmed in writing	
Number of guests	
Time of arrival at venue	
Time of departure from venue	
When is access available before the reception?	
What are the arrangements for clearing away/locking up?	
Is smoking allowed?	
Is there a licence to serve alcohol?	
Parking facilities	
Cloakroom/toilet facilities	
Bar facilities	
Kitchen facilities	
Tables/chairs available?	
What do we need to hire separately?	

Heating requested	
Where will flowers be put?	
Who will supply them?	
Other decorations	
Who will arrange the flowers and decorations?	
Where will gifts be displayed?	
Where will bride and groom change?	
Is a room available for children?	
What does the cost include?	
VAT	£
TOTAL COST	£
Deposit paid	£
Balance due	£

Hiring a marquee

Those who wish to hold their reception at home but who do not have enough space inside the house can hire a marquee. You need a large open space to accommodate a marquee, and this option can be as expensive as holding the reception at a hotel (depending on the size and quality of the marquee). Marquees are ideal in late spring, summer and early autumn but you can have one in winter as long as you have adequate heating. At any time of the year you should make plans in case of wet weather. If you choose this option you have to arrange catering, drinks, decorations etc. yourself.

Marquee checklist

Name of supplier	
Address	
Telephone/fax/email	
Contact	
Date booking made	
Confirmed in writing	
Size	
Number of guests	
When will the marquee be erected?	
Electricity supply	
Flowers and decorations	
When will the marquee be removed?	
Cost of marquee	£
Extras booked	
Lining	£
Coconut matting	£
Dance floor	£
Spotlights	£
Chandeliers	£
Heating	£
Tables and chairs (no.)	£
Portable toilets	£
Other	£
VAT	£
TOTAL COST	£
Deposit paid	£
Balance due	£

The caterers will work in an adjoining tent (so allow for this when working out how much space you need for the marquee) and may need access to the kitchen in the house. Choose a caterer who has worked in a marquee before. You will also have to make sure that the marquee supplier provides enough electricity for the caterers to cook and run a fridge. Once you have decided on your menu, the caterers will be able to tell you what equipment they will be using; you can then pass this information to the marquee supplier, who can then arrange the correct electricity supply. The marquee is usually put up three or four days before the event.

Checkpoints for hiring a marquee:

- if you are having the marquee in your garden, warn neighbours in advance about the influx of guests, noise levels and increase in demand for parking
- make sure you have allowed sufficient space for guests to assemble for a drink before the main reception
- it is useful, particularly in cold or wet weather, to be able to walk straight out of your house into the marquee. It is ideal if you have French windows that can open directly into the marquee, but if you don't the marquee provider can construct a covered walkway from one of the doors of the house
- extras, which add to the cost of the marquee, include: lining, coconut matting, dance floor, chandelier lighting, heating, tables and chairs, portable toilets
- you will have to pay VAT but may be able to save on the overall cost by booking well in advance
- if you want hanging baskets, the marquee provider can instal ropes from which to hang them
- a 25 per cent deposit is usually requested on booking and is non-returnable.

Holding the reception in your home

Home-based receptions involve a lot of work for the organisers but can have a very relaxed and informal atmosphere. The cost is relatively low, especially if you produce the food yourself. If you do not want to take on the job of feeding everyone, you can hire a caterer.

Checkpoints for having the reception at home:

- be realistic about the number of people you can accommodate in comfort

- check whether you have enough crockery, tables etc. If not, you may be able to borrow or hire them
- if you are going to hire caterers, make sure you have adequate facilities for them
- enlist lots of help from family and friends and delegate as much as you can
- tell neighbours well in advance about the increase in noise levels and demand for parking.

Home checklist

Number of guests	
Parking arrangements	
Which rooms will be used?	
Cloakroom/toilet facilities	
What arrangements have been made for flowers and other decorations?	
What items do we need to hire?	
Who will help?	

The food

Having decided on the venue, the next decisions you need to make are what sort of food to serve and who will prepare it. If you are using a hotel or restaurant, the food will be prepared as part of the overall package, and you will be offered a choice of menus for different types of meal, each priced per head. For other venues you will probably want to use an outside caterer.

Choosing a caterer

Book early, but not until you have compared various services and received several estimates. Personal recommendation is always preferable, otherwise you should follow up references from any caterers you are considering. Once you have chosen a caterer, you will need to supply the following information:

- the date and time of your reception
- the facilities available at the location
- the budget per head and estimated number of guests
- the kind of meal you would like
- whether any guests have special dietary requirements (although this information may not be available until you have had replies from all your guests)
- whether you would like them to supply champagne and wine (see pages 183–5).

Most caterers will supply you with a number of sample menus to choose from and should be able to add any other dishes that you particularly want. Check whether the price includes:

- tables and chairs
- table linen
- crockery, cutlery and glasses
- flowers
- serving staff
- cloakroom attendants
- clearing up after the event.

Also check whether:

- for a buffet, you are being charged per person or per plate. Some caterers charge extra for second helpings
- bread, for example, is charged as an extra
- you are expected to pay for the catering staff to have a meal during the reception
- VAT is included
- tips are expected, or a service charge is added to the fee.

Sort out all these points before you confirm the price, both verbally and then in writing. Tell the caterers of any last-minute additions or deletions to the guest list. You will be expected to pay for the number of meals ordered, even if on the day some guests do not attend.

What sort of food?

When choosing the food for your reception, remember that, particularly with large numbers of people, you are catering for a wide range of tastes. If you want to choose some adventurous options, make sure you also include other dishes that appeal across the board. It is wise to include a vegetarian option as well, and some plainer food for children.

Sit-down meal

This is the most formal, and most expensive, option. Although it provides a welcome opportunity for guests to sit down, it also limits their chances to mingle, due to the constraints of a seating plan (see pages 188–9). For a reception that continues for several hours, a sit-down meal provides a good opportunity for guests to relax before the entertainment begins.

Buffet meal

A buffet meal can be cheaper than a sit-down meal as you need only one or two people to serve the food from the main table (unlike a sit-down meal, where you need a number of people to serve at each table). If you prefer, guests could help themselves. Buffet food can be just as substantial as a sit-down meal, but it is perhaps easier to provide a wider choice, such as a vegetarian option, a fish dish and a meat dish, with a variety of vegetables and salads. Guests can then choose exactly what they like. You could arrange a seating plan or let guests find their own seats once they have selected their food. At a large reception, it could take 30 minutes for guests to be served from a buffet.

Canapés and finger buffets

Trays of canapés and cocktail snacks can be taken round by catering staff and offered to guests. Choose foods that are easily managed with fingers if the food is to be eaten standing and serve everything in bite-sized portions, avoiding foods that crumble or drip.

For a finger buffet choose eight to ten different canapés and budget for 12 or more pieces per head. Cold foods are the easiest option, but a few hot items are always welcome. Hot canapés can be greasy, so serve them on sticks or mini forks and provide napkins. If serving them straight from trays, ensure that hot items are offered at a temperature suitable for eating immediately.

Tip

Double-check the portion sizes with caterers and err on the side of generosity. There is nothing worse than a buffet that runs out before everyone has been served.

Hiring a caterer checklist

Name of caterer	
Address	
Telephone/fax/email	
Contact	
Date booking made	
Confirmed in writing	
Number of guests to be served	
Number of children's portions	
What dishes are being served?	
Any special dietary requirements?	
Number of serving staff	
Does the cost include:	
Tables and chairs	
Table linen	
Crockery, cutlery and glasses	
Flowers	

Ovens	
Refrigerators	
Serving staff	
Cloakroom attendants	
Clearing up	
Are the caterers providing drinks? If so, what types and amounts are agreed?	
Corkage charge	£
How and when will caterers get access?	
Electricity supply needed	
Cost per head of food	£
Cost of drink	£
Extra costs (itemise)	
Service charge	£
Tips	£
VAT	£
TOTAL COST	£

Catering at home

Tackle this only if you are sure that you – or your friends and family – are happy to take on this extra task at an already busy time. If you feel you can cope, this is a good way to save money. Start the preparations well in advance and ask your neighbours and friends if they have any spare freezer-capacity. Unless you are an accomplished caterer, go for simplicity.

You will also need to be able to make tea or coffee for your guests, so make sure you have the means to do this and hire anything you are lacking, for example a large urn for heating water, extra crockery or perhaps a large coffee filter machine. Remember to enlist people to help with setting up as well as clearing up, both during and after the reception. Keep a list of who is doing what, who has loaned what and what has been hired.

You will need a large table to lay out the buffet. Arrange the food in a logical order, either starting at one end and working down to the other, or starting at both ends and working towards the centre. Place plates, cutlery and napkins at the starting points.

One month or more before the wedding

- Finalise menu and start making any dishes that can be frozen.
- Make notes while you are preparing the food of anything needed for serving, such as garnishes or cream.
- Arrange to borrow or hire any equipment you need.

A week before the wedding

- Double-check that you have everything you need and confirm orders for hired items and drinks.
- Order bread for delivery/collection on the day.
- Make any dishes that can be refrigerated until needed.
- Two days before, buy perishables such as cheese, salads, fruit and cream.

The day before

- Take frozen dishes out of the freezer.
- Lay the buffet table and put out glasses, crockery and cutlery.

On the day

- Ask someone who is not going to the wedding to garnish the food and set it out on the table no more than two hours before it is to be eaten. Leave chilled dishes in refrigerator until shortly before serving.
- Prepare the salads.
- Chill wines.
- Arrange hot dishes ready for reheating.
- Dress salads just before serving.

Catering at home checklist

Number of adult guests				
Number of children				
Food				
Dishes chosen				
Any special dietary needs				

Dish	No. of portions	Who will prepare it?	Where will it be stored?	What is needed to serve it?

Other foods needed (bread, dressings etc.)			

Crockery, cutlery etc.	How many are needed?	Borrow/ hire	Who from?

Setting out, serving, clearing away

Task	When should it be done?	Who will do it?

The drink

If you have decided to hold your reception at a hotel or restaurant the drinks will almost certainly be provided as part of the overall package, and you will need to discuss which wines to serve when you make the catering arrangements.

If you are using caterers at home or at another venue they may also provide the wine, but it could be worth your while doing some cost comparisons, as you might be able to save money by providing the wine yourself. Caterers usually charge a corkage fee for handling and serving the drinks if you do this, but they may provide glasses and ice. It pays to check corkage fees carefully, as they can make a serious dent in any savings you make by buying your own wines. Although some venues and caterers do not impose a fee, the majority do charge you for the privilege of providing your own drink. The amount charged per bottle varies widely, but you're unlikely to be asked for less than £5, and quotes of £8 per bottle and upwards are not unusual.

For a hired venue such as a hall or stately home, check that it has a licence to consume alcohol; if not, you can apply for a temporary (occasional) licence from the magistrate's court.

On arrival

It is usual to serve guests with a drink as soon as they arrive at the reception or have been greeted by the receiving line. Champagne, buck's fizz, sparkling wine or a choice of medium or dry sherry are all traditional, but a glass of red or white wine – or, in winter, mulled wine – would also be acceptable. Non-alcoholic drinks should be available throughout the reception for drivers, non-drinkers and children; these could include fruit juices, mineral water, soft drinks both fizzy and still and, if you like, non-alcoholic wines and beers.

With the meal

You can limit the choice by serving sparkling wine, or even champagne if your budget can stretch to it, throughout the proceedings. Alternatively, you can serve a choice of red or white wine throughout the meal.

For the toasts

Champagne is the traditional choice, but many excellent sparkling wines are much cheaper.

After the meal

Most guests appreciate tea or coffee at the end of the meal. If the reception is going on into the evening you can continue to serve wine and non-alcoholic drinks or let guests choose their own drinks from the bar, if there is one. You can either foot the bill throughout the evening or pay for drinks up to a prearranged limit, after which guests buy their own. During a reception that goes on for several hours in the evening, it is a good idea to offer tea or coffee again, midway through the proceedings.

Providing the drinks yourself

This is a money-saving option if you are holding the reception at a hired venue or at home. Shop around local off-licences. Most will offer champagne and wine on a sale-or-return basis. You could also consider buying from a supermarket, especially if you have time to wait for a suitable offer to appear.

If you live near a Channel port and have the time, it could be worthwhile buying your wine and champagne in France. Do some research before you go, and take a detailed shopping list with you – it is easy to get carried away, and the object is to end up making a saving. Take account of the cost of travel, plus the fact that you won't be able to make a sale-or-return deal, so will need to be able to use everything you buy. Check websites★ for useful information about day trips to France. You can order online at Sainsburys in Calais★.

Off-licences will often deliver the wine and supply glasses free if you order all your drink from them. You may even be able to return the glasses unwashed – it is certainly worth asking, as this can be a big chore. Hire enough glasses for one-and-a-half times the number of guests. For a reception held at home, put one or two people in charge of serving the drinks. At a hired venue you could consider hiring the services of a bartender, but check his or her references before booking.

Your off-licence or local supermarket may sell ice, or you might find a supplier who can deliver ice on the day through the *Yellow Pages*. To chill white wine and champagne, float bottles in plastic rubbish bins filled with ice and water. One case of wine takes an hour to cool, and you can move chilled bottles to the top of the bins and put more in underneath as you start to use them. Still white wine can be opened ahead of time, and the corks pushed gently back in until the wine is needed.

Providing the drinks yourself checklist

	What will be served?	Quantity	Cost
On arrival			
With the meal			
For the toasts			
After the meal			
Total cost of drinks	£		
Cost of glass hire	£		
Corkage	£		
Ice	£		
Bar staff	£		
Other costs			
TOTAL COST	£		

Estimating quantities

One bottle of wine or champagne serves six glasses, or twelve if it is being mixed with orange juice for buck's fizz. During a reception lasting three hours each guest will, on average, consume half a bottle of wine. This allows for those who drink far less than this. If the reception is going on for longer you should increase this allowance accordingly. It is always better to overestimate (if you buy on a sale-or-return basis, you can always get a refund if you have any drink left over).

Hiring a toastmaster

For a formal wedding with a large number of guests you could consider hiring a toastmaster. Hotels will be able to organise this for you, or you may find someone suitable through the *Yellow Pages* or the Guild of International Toastmasters★. A toastmaster announces the guests as they arrive, makes an announcement when the meal is to be served, introduces the speech-makers, announces the cake-cutting ceremony and tells guests what the order of events will be afterwards. The best man or another male guest can be asked to perform these tasks instead if you prefer.

Reception stationery and decorations

You can personalise your reception with printed items, ranging from menus, place cards, napkins and coasters to matchbooks, napkin rings and favours. You will find a wide range of designs at stationers or specialist printers, who advertise in bridal magazines, or look at wedding websites (page 233) for ideas. Order items about three months before the wedding day. You can save money by writing menus and place cards by hand on plain white or coloured card, or by designing them yourself on a computer (see page 68). You can buy favours such as little boxes of sugared almonds from chain-store bridal departments or confectioners. For information on where to use flowers at the reception, see page 114. Other decorations, such as banners or balloons, can be printed with your names and the date of the wedding. An evening could end with fireworks if the venue is suitable. Look in the *Yellow Pages* for companies who can put on a display.

Chapter 20

At the reception

All the rules of traditional wedding etiquette are explained in this chapter, but none of them are carved in stone. Perhaps the bride wants to give a speech, or the groom would like his sister to act as 'best woman'. It can be done. Perhaps you are in a situation where traditional etiquette does not fit. Couples marrying for the second time, those who have children whom they would like to include, those whose parents are divorced or those who just want a very informal and personal occasion can organise the occasion in whatever way is most likely to keep everyone happy.

When planning your reception, it is vital to work out a careful timetable. Allow enough time for all the guests to arrive, be greeted and mingle while having a drink, but do not keep them waiting too long before the meal is served. Allow for the meal to be served and eaten unhurriedly, then add some time for the speeches, toasts and cutting the cake. If you are leaving the reception at this point, the guests can mingle again while you get changed, and can then say their goodbyes. Otherwise, give an interval for people to move around and stretch their legs before they are seated again for any entertainment and dancing. Remember that the reception might start late if the ceremony overruns, so build some contingency time into your timetable, just in case. You can delegate someone to be 'in charge' of the reception on the day and give him or her a list of contact numbers for all suppliers involved, and a detailed timetable. See page 31 for reception etiquette at second marriages.

The receiving line

At a formal wedding you can have a full receiving line to greet guests as they arrive. If you are using a toastmaster he can announce the name of each guest. The traditional order for the receiving line is:

- bride's mother
- bride's father
- groom's mother
- groom's father
- bride
- groom
- best man (if he arrives at the reception from the church in time)
- chief bridesmaid.

Time spent talking to each guest should be kept brief, otherwise guests will have to queue. To prevent delays, and to give a more informal start to the reception, the two of you could greet the guests on your own or you could circulate among them as they arrive, making sure you talk to everyone present. You could ask guests to sign a wedding book (see page 87) at this point.

Q *My parents divorced acrimoniously years ago and refuse to speak to each other, never mind stand together in the receiving line. What shall I do?*

A For a formal receiving line, they could stand in the following order: bride's mother, groom's father, bride's father, groom's mother. However, it is probably best to dispense with a formal receiving line altogether and greet the guests without your parents, who can mingle separately.

Seating plans

If you are having a sit-down meal (or perhaps a buffet) you will need to give some thought to a seating plan. Traditionally, the newly-weds sit with their families at the top table, sitting in the following order, from left to right facing the table:

- chief bridesmaid
- groom's father
- bride's mother
- groom
- bride
- bride's father
- groom's mother
- best man.

Although this is the convention, you can alter it to suit your needs, perhaps including another family member to partner an unaccompanied parent, for instance, or changing the positions of the best man and chief bridesmaid.

Q *My parents are divorced and remarried. How do I organise the seating plan for the top table?*

A If the wedding is being hosted by your parents, you could stick with the convention and seat your parents at the top table and your step-parents at other tables close by among the other guests. If everyone gets along reasonably well there is no reason why both parents and step-parents should not be seated at the top table.

As far as the other tables are concerned, people closest to the bride and groom should sit nearest the top table. The rule is that married couples do not sit together at wedding receptions, but rules are made to be broken and you should seat people where you think they will be happiest. It is a good idea to mix up groups of say, friends and work colleagues among relatives and other guests during the meal, especially if the reception is going on into the evening, so that guests can meet new people, and friends will have a chance to catch up with each other later on. If the meal is the only opportunity people will have to socialise, you could seat friends nearer to each other.

Be especially thoughtful when seating people who have come on their own or who know very few people at the reception and place them next to someone who can be relied on to include them in the conversation.

Tip

Do not write out the master seating plan, which will be displayed on the day, too early as guests may drop out at the last minute or ask if they can bring someone extra along. If this happens you may have to swap a lot of people round to accommodate the changes and perhaps write out the seating plan a second time.

Tom and Mandy

The only hiccup on Tom and Mandy's wedding day was that the hotel laid out the tables to a completely different plan from that agreed.

'We'd been offered a choice of two table layouts to accommodate our 100 guests. We'd chosen one and then spent hours working out who was sitting next to whom. When we walked into the dining room after the wedding and all the guests had taken their places we found the tables were facing the wrong way, so we did not have the view of the sea we'd wanted from the top table, and guests who were supposed to be sitting right next to the top table were as far away as was possible. Not only did the hotel not apologise, but they said that they could not fit everyone in using the configuration we'd asked for – which was one that they had originally suggested. My advice would be to double-check that everyone can be seated as you would like before you spend any time on the detailed seating plan, and confirm the arrangements a couple of days before.'

Toasts and speeches

As guests reach the end of the meal, the toastmaster, or best man if he is acting as master of ceremonies, asks for silence so that the speeches may be made. Some couples like to cut the cake before the speeches so that it can be sliced into portions while the speeches are being made and served with coffee immediately afterwards. Otherwise, you can have the cake-cutting ceremony afterwards.

The main purpose of the speeches is to thank publicly everyone who has contributed to the success of the day; to introduce the toasts to the bride and groom and bridesmaids; to entertain the guests briefly with thoughts on marriage, reminiscences about the bride and groom and so on. The best speeches are brief. None should last much more than five minutes, and three minutes would be plenty for the bride's father and groom.

If you are nervous at the prospect of making a speech, remember that the guests will be warmly disposed towards you, and the happy atmosphere on the day will help to carry you along. A sincere speech, even if it is quite brief, will be well received. That said, no one who feels that the prospect of making a speech would ruin their day should be made to do so. If this applies to you, you could decide to give the very briefest of thanks before proposing the toast or even ask someone else who enjoys public speaking to give the speech in your place. See page 32 for advice on speeches at second marriages.

The bride's father

He is the first to speak and should keep his speech fairly brief and to the point. If, for any reason, the bride's father is not present, the person who gave her away, or another close relative, can be asked to give the speech instead. In his speech the bride's father should:

- greet the guests and thank them for coming
- congratulate the groom and welcome him into the family, per-haps also mentioning the groom's parents
- end the speech by proposing a toast to the bride and groom. This can be made to 'the bride and groom', 'the happy couple' or he can use the couple's names.

During his speech, the bride's father can talk about the pleasure he has had from raising his daughter and include one or two anecdotes about her childhood or growing up. He can also offer the couple advice on marriage, speaking from his own experience, if he wishes.

The groom

The groom replies to the toast on behalf of the bride and himself. His speech may be a little longer than that of the bride's father. He should:

- thank the bride's father for the toast. He should also thank the bride's parents for allowing him to marry their daughter and, if applicable, for their generosity in hosting the wedding
- thank the guests for attending the wedding and for their gifts
- say something about his good fortune in meeting his bride and his confidence in their future happiness together. He can include one or two anecdotes about their courtship if he wishes
- mention his own parents and thank them for all they have done for him, both in bringing him up and in helping with the wedding preparations

- give special thanks to everyone who has helped with the wedding day, mentioning in particular any friends or family members who have made a special contribution, and the best man
- finally, praise the bridesmaids for their role during the day and propose the toast saying either, 'to the bridesmaids' or using their names.

The best man

The best man makes the final speech. He can speak for a little longer than the other two and can include one or two jokes or amusing anecdotes, bearing in mind his audience, which is likely to range from children to elderly relatives. However, he can also take the opportunity to say something more serious about his relationship with the groom and what it means to him. He should:

- thank the groom for the toast on behalf of the bridesmaids
- congratulate the newly-wed couple
- thank anyone connected with the wedding who has given him particular help
- end his speech with a toast to the bride and groom
- finally, read out any telemessages, emails or cards that have been received, first vetting them for unsuitable comments. If there are a great many he could read one or two messages and list the names of other senders

Q *Can the bride make a speech? I don't like the idea of sitting in silence and would love the opportunity to say thank you as well for all the help we have had in the run up to the wedding.*

A There is no reason why you shouldn't make a speech, and an increasing number of brides choose to do so. You can speak before the groom and ask your father to give you an introduction, or after the groom, before the toast to the bridesmaids, which means the groom will have to stand again to make the toast. Otherwise you could make your speech a little later in the proceedings, after the cake has been cut and before guests rise and move into a different room. Your speech can be similar in tone to the groom's, thanking your family and the guests, and saying something affectionate about your new husband.

How to write and deliver a good speech

- The key to giving a good speech is to **plan it in advance**.
- **Don't write the speech out and read it word for word**, as this will make your delivery stilted. Instead, write key points with a few memory-jogging phrases for each on a series of numbered cards, which can be kept in your pocket until they are needed. Practise the speech beforehand so that it becomes very familiar, then use the cards as prompts to guide you through the speech. This method also allows you to improvise or add to the speech if something occurs to you on the day and will help to make the speech sound more spontaneous.
- **Organise your speech so that it gets off to a lively start and engages the audience's attention**. The middle section should be the longest, and you should conclude with a neat lead in to the toast at the end.
- **Make a special note of all the people you have to thank**, with links or brief anecdotes next to them.
- **Read out the draft of your speech and time it**. Then leave the draft for a day or two before looking at it again.
- **Keep the speech short and to the point** without being brusque. Don't tell long-winded jokes or anecdotes. Brief stories, which arrive quickly at their point, are the best.
- **Be careful about jokes**, especially if you are making them at someone else's expense. It is acceptable for the best man to raise a laugh at the groom's expense if it is done affectionately, but you should steer clear of humorous references to the bride's mother or the bride. Jokes should be kept clean and mild. One-liners are often more effective than longer jokes.
- You can learn a lot about how to improve your delivery simply by **taping the speech and listening to it carefully**. You can also try it out on trusted friends and judge the effect of any jokes or anecdotes you plan to use.
- On the day, **do not have more than a couple of drinks before making your speech**. When the moment comes, try to relax, take a few steadying breaths before you rise, and smile at your audience as you begin to speak.
- **Stand naturally, with your hands at your sides, or in front of you holding your prompt cards**. Do not grasp your lapels or lean forward with your hands resting on the table.

- When delivering the speech **aim to sound neither pompous nor overly informal**. Even at a very relaxed reception a certain level of formality is appropriate for the speeches. Use everyday language rather than formal expressions but avoid slang and clichés.

- **Use your normal voice, not an assumed accent or 'stage' voice**. Keep your head up and speak clearly and not too fast.

- **Remember to breathe normally, and pause slightly between sentences to breathe**. People often 'forget' to breathe when they are nervous, and you can find yourself running out of breath towards the end of a sentence.

- **Keep your gaze just above the heads of your audience** and do not stare round at doors, windows or the ceiling. When mentioning anyone specifically or proposing a toast you should look towards the person concerned without staring or making them feel uncomfortable.

- Get some inspiration from a **book or website**, but don't be tempted to copy a speech verbatim. If you prefer to write a speech from scratch, search for suitable quotations, anecdotes and jokes both for weddings and for after-dinner speeches to weave in among stories of your own.

Cutting the cake

Once the speeches and toasts are over, the best man, or toastmaster, announces the cutting of the cake. The bride holds the cake knife and the groom puts his hands over hers to make the first cut. It is helpful if the cut has been discreetly started beforehand, so that you do not have to struggle to get the knife through hard icing. Photographs are usually taken at this point. One cut is all that is needed, then the cake is taken away and cut into small portions which are distributed by the bridesmaids and pages or by the waiters and waitresses.

Entertainment

You can arrange background music – either live or recorded – while the guests are arriving and eating. At a longer reception, you will also need music for dancing in the evening. Remember that it will take about 45 minutes for a band or disco to set up.

Ask for recommendations and look on websites, wedding maga-zines and in the *Yellow Pages*. Try to attend a performance, or at least listen to a recording, by any musicians you are considering hiring before booking them and discuss the sort of music you have in mind to make sure it is within their range. The cost will depend on:

- how many players are involved
- how busy they are
- how long you want them to play for
- how far they have to travel
- whether you ask them to learn any new items specially for the occasion.

Confirm in writing details of the date, venue, amount payable, can-cellation policy, length of time for playing and for breaks.

Orchestras, bands and groups

Hiring an orchestra or band is ideal if you have a large number of guests and want dancing to live music. Most musicians who play regularly at weddings have a suitable repertoire, which should be varied in order to appeal to the wide age range at the wedding. A barn dance or ceilidh are other options, for which you can use recorded or live music, but you would need to hire a caller to direct the dances.

You should find out what the musicians' policy on taking breaks is. Do they provide recorded music to be played while they are hav-ing their breaks or do they let one person at a time rest while the others continue playing? You will probably want some form of music to fill in the gaps if the musicians do have their breaks at the same time, so it is best to know in advance if you have to make your own arrangements for this.

Ensembles and soloists

These are good for background music at a smaller venue or in addi-tion to dance music at a large reception. You could choose a pianist, flautist, harpist, string ensemble, jazz musicians, steel band, fiddlers, medieval minstrels or singers.

Recorded music, discos and DJs

Live entertainment is not cheap, and you can keep costs down by using recorded background music. A hotel may have suitable

CDs and a sound system. At other venues you can put together your own recorded music and ask a friend to play it over your own sound system or one which has been hired or borrowed. You can provide dance music in the same way.

Using a DJ who provides a sound system and selection of music is another good way to entertain your guests and is cheaper than using live musicians. Make sure the DJ knows the types of music you want and understands that the volume must not be too loud.

Dancing

Traditionally, the bride and groom dance alone together for a few minutes before other guests join in. During the evening the bride should dance with all the men in the family party, and the groom with the women. The best man should also dance with the women of the wedding party, including the bride. In the intervals between dances the couple should circulate together and separately and make sure they speak to everyone present, taking the opportunity to thank any who have been particularly helpful towards making the day a success.

Suitable music for the first dance

- 'Let's Stay Together' sung by Al Green
- 'When a Man Loves a Woman' sung by Percy Sledge
- 'The First Time Ever I Saw Your Face' sung by Roberta Flack
- 'How Deep Is Your Love ' sung by Take That
- 'We've Only Just Begun' sung by The Carpenters
- 'Wonderful World' sung by Louis Armstrong
- 'My Heart Will Go On' sung by Celine Dion.

Entertainment for children

If you are having a large number of children at your wedding reception, it could be worthwhile arranging entertainment specifically for them. If your budget allows, you could hire a professional entertainer, who could also look after them during the ceremony (look in the *Yellow Pages*). Otherwise, you could arrange for a few helpers to keep an eye on the children while they are playing in a separate room. The parents might be able to help on a rota basis, so that no one misses too much of the reception.

Entertainment possibilities include:

- **a professional children's entertainer** – a clown, magician, Punch and Judy or other puppet show. Some entertainers offer party packages which are intended for children's birthday parties but could be adapted for a wedding
- **a bouncy castle**
- **a children's disco**
- **a selection of videos** for the children to watch. Feature-length cartoons are popular
- some companies, such as the Wedding Crèche Service★, offer an '**activity crèche**' service, where children are looked after for you and kept occupied with toys, games, storytelling, music, face painting, playdough and crayons or even gym equipment.

Leaving the reception

Towards the end of the festivities the best man should tell you when it is time to change. The chief bridesmaid can help the bride, and she or the bride's mother can take charge of the bride's dress. The best man takes care of the groom's clothes, returning any hired clothes by the agreed date.

The best man makes sure your transport is ready and announces that you are ready to leave. The guests gather at the door and may throw confetti or flower petals. The bride tosses her bouquet, or a posy of flowers removed from it, into the crowd, and everyone follows the couple outside to give them a final send-off as they drive or are driven away. The couple's departure is the signal for the guests to begin leaving, and indeed no one should have left before this. This does not apply if the party goes on until the early hours of the morning and the couple plan to stay until the end. If this is the case, it would be a good idea for the best man to announce their plans during the speeches.

Now is the time to settle the bill and check that nothing has been left behind by guests. The bride's parents, best man or chief bridesmaid remove the remains of the cake, the couple's wedding clothes, telemessages, emails and cards and any flowers which they would like to take home. They also arrange for the wedding gifts to be taken somewhere for safe keeping until the couple return from honeymoon. The hosts and best man are the last to leave the reception.

Entertainment checklist

Name of musicians for background music	
Address	
Telephone/fax/email	
Contact	
Date booked	
Confirmed in writing	
Arrival time	
Play from:	To:
Breaks agreed	
Where will the musicians perform?	
Particular items requested to be played	
COST	£
Deposit paid	£
Balance due	£
Name of musicians/DJ for dance music	
Address	
Telephone/fax/email	
Contact	
Date booked	
Confirmed in writing	
Arrival time	
Play from:	To:
Breaks agreed	
Where will the musicians perform?	

Particular items requested to be played	
COST	£
Deposit paid	£
Balance due	£

Name of children's entertainer

Address	
Telephone/fax/email	
Contact	
Date booked	
Confirmed in writing	
Entertainment agreed	
Arrival time	
Entertain from:	To:
Breaks agreed	
Where will the entertainment take place?	
VAT	
COST	£
Deposit paid	£
Balance due	£

Chapter 21

Insurance

When you are planning your big day, insurance will probably not be at the top of your list of things to organise, but it is worth setting some time aside to check that you will not lose out financially if anything goes wrong.

Whether or not you choose to buy one of the specialist wedding policies depends on how much money you will be investing in your wedding and the kind of mishap you are worried about. You should also bear in mind that while wedding insurance covers you up to – and including – the day itself, it does not cover you afterwards. So since you may be making large purchases (such as engagement and wedding rings) several months before the wedding and you will have your rings and wedding presents for a long time afterwards, you should check that your existing house contents insurance covers you for these things.

Do you need wedding insurance?

The main reason for buying wedding insurance is to cover yourself against the cost of having to cancel or reschedule your wedding. So whether this sort of insurance is worthwhile depends to a large extent on the cancellation fees your suppliers will charge you and whether they will waive the fees if you subsequently reschedule the wedding.

A wedding insurance policy will not cover you if you have to cancel simply because either of you has had a change of heart, or reimburse you if you knew you were going to cancel (or you knew about something – a close relative's illness, for example – that might cause you to cancel) before you took out the insurance. However, in the main you will find that you can buy cover against unforeseen disasters that cause you to cancel, such as:

- the death, illness or injury of the bride, groom or a close relative – but check the definition of 'close relative' carefully because it varies from policy to policy
- the inability of one of the above to attend the wedding because of jury service, redundancy, cancelled leave (if in the Armed Forces) or, with some policies, extreme weather conditions (such as being snowed in and unable to get to the wedding as a result)
- failure of suppliers (e.g. florists, caterers, wedding cars, photographers and so on) because they have gone out of business – but note that you will not be covered if a supplier simply fails to meet the terms of your contract and is still in business. This is because you can sue instead (see 'When things go wrong' on page 206)
- the ceremony or reception venue no longer being available for you to use
- being unable to find replacements for lost or damaged wedding dress, hired suits and bridesmaids' dresses.

Tip

The best insurance against failure of suppliers to deliver is to choose reputable firms, to ensure that you have a clear written agreement and – if possible – to avoid making full and final payment until after the delivery of goods and services.

You will also find that most policies will pay out:

- for the cost of arranging alternative transport because the wedding car did not turn up
- if you managed to avoid cancelling the wedding by getting a different supplier to do the job – the most you can claim is typically 25 per cent of the original supplier's invoice
- for loss of deposits you have paid to suppliers who fail to deliver goods or services (because they have gone out of business)
- for the loss of deposits paid for live entertainment if the entertainment does not arrive (for whatever reason)
- for replacing or repairing the wedding rings (but not the engagement ring), wedding clothes (of key people) and wedding presents if they are lost, stolen or damaged (although you may already have this cover – see 'Cover outside the home' on page 204)

- if you need to re-stage the wedding to take photographs or record a video because the original film or negatives were lost or damaged (however, no policy will pay out to re-stage the photography just because you were disappointed with the original results)
- for the legal expenses involved in defending your case if you are sued by a supplier for damage you or one of your guests caused or – less probably – if a guest sues you. (However, if you are holding your reception at home, your legal liability if people injure themselves when visiting you is already covered by your contents insurance – see page 204)
- if you hire a marquee and your supplier tells you that you are responsible for insuring against damage to it. Note that this cover may be offered as an add-on for which you will have to pay more.

Tip

If you know you would not want to re-stage your wedding just for the photographs but would be disappointed if you had no record of your big day, consider appointing a friend who is good at photography to step into the breach if the need arises. Alternatively, ask your wedding guests for copies of photos they may have taken.

Buying wedding insurance

The most important consideration when buying this kind of insurance is to make sure you buy sufficient cover. After all, there is little point buying a policy which will pay out a maximum of only £3,000 if the cost of cancelling your wedding would actually be, say, £8,000. You should also check that other limits in the policy – e.g. what will be paid for re-staging photographs or damage to wedding attire – are sufficient to cover your particular wedding arrangements.

If you are offered wedding insurance by one of your suppliers, do not take it until you have compared both the cover and price with policies offered elsewhere. Policies do vary – some automatically include cover for damage to marquees, for example, while others charge extra for this kind of cover.

The price of this kind of insurance varies too. For example, to cover cancellation costs of £6,000, you could pay as little as £50 or as much as £125 – while insuring against costs of £10,000 could set you back from £100 to as much as £300.

You can get a comprehensive list of insurers and intermediaries selling wedding insurance, together with links to their websites, and a prewritten email for requesting details at the WedUK website★.

Why you should check your existing insurance

There are two main reasons for looking at your existing insurance:

- to see whether you really need to buy special wedding insurance (see pages 200–202)
- to make sure that you have sufficient insurance for those things that a special wedding policy will not cover.

Cover for valuables

It is unlikely that you will find wedding insurance that will cover your engagement ring, and you will also find that the wedding rings are covered only if they are lost or damaged in the week leading up to the wedding. So as soon as the engagement and/or wedding rings have been bought, you should make sure that your existing contents insurance provides enough cover in case they are lost, damaged or stolen. Many contents policies have what are called 'single item' limits for valuable belongings – £1,000, for example – although it might be lower or higher. The limit represents the most that will be paid out in the event of a claim, even if the cost of replacing each ring is more than your insurer's single-item limit. You should also check the limit if your wedding dress is particularly costly.

Tip

Make sure that you keep the receipt for each ring since it may be needed as evidence if you do ever have to claim for its loss. If you want to have your ring professionally valued for insurance purposes, go to a jeweller who is a member of the Incorporated Society of Valuers and Auctioneers (ISVA). Whether your ring is antique or new, it is a good idea to take a photograph of it (this will help to identify it if it is ever stolen).

Cover outside the home

Because you will be wearing your ring(s) when you are away from home, it is worth finding out whether you have 'all risks' cover (sometimes called 'cover away from the home'). If you do not already have this cover, expect to pay more for your insurance and note that there may be a different single-item limit, so check that too. The advantage of buying an all-risks extension to your contents policy is that your belongings are usually covered when you are abroad, and some insurers will give you a discount on your travel insurance, which could be useful for the honeymoon.

It is also worthwhile checking your insurer's single-item limits and all-risks cover if you are expecting to receive particularly valuable engagement and wedding presents. This is especially important if you plan to put them on display at the reception: if you do not have all-risks cover, you may not be able to claim if something happens to them on the way to the reception venue – although this is less of a problem if your reception is held at home.

Tip

If you are getting married abroad, it is unlikely that standard travel insurance will provide the level of cover you will need to replace your rings, the wedding dress (and other wedding clothes) and any wedding presents that may be sent to you which fail to arrive at your destination or get stolen. So in addition to travel insurance, you should make sure you arrange an all-risks extension to your contents policy (which will provide better cover for your belongings than travel insurance).

Checking your contents policy

You may also need to increase the total amount you have your home contents insured for (to include your rings and presents). Some house contents policies automatically provide extra cover for wedding presents, but for a limited amount of time only – 30 days each side of the wedding day, for example, but check your policy to make sure. With other policies, you will need to increase your cover and possibly pay a higher premium. If you are getting married in your parents' home town and a large number of presents are being brought to your wedding, it is likely that you will need your parents to look after these presents until you get back from your honeymoon. If this is the case, you will need to check your parents' house contents policy as well as your own.

Tip

If your reception is to be held at home – and especially if you are hiring outside suppliers – it is worth informing your existing insurers that this will be the case. If anything is damaged or goes missing during the reception, your insurers could refuse to pay any claims you make on the grounds that you did not tell them that there were going to be a large number of people in the house.

Insurance for the honeymoon

If you are planning to go abroad for your honeymoon, you will need to organise travel insurance. The main reason for buying travel insurance is to cover yourself against the costs of emergency medical treatment while you are abroad and the potentially very expensive bill if you are legally required to pay damages to someone whose property you have damaged or whom you have injured while on your travels. You also need additional cover for cancellation, delayed or missed departure, legal expenses and personal accident. However, if you already have an all-risks extension to your house contents policy, you may not need a travel policy to cover your money and belongings and you may be able to get a discount on your travel insurance.

You also need to check that your policy covers you for taking part in any dangerous activities – scuba diving or white-water rafting, for example. However, what you consider dangerous and what your insurer considers dangerous may differ so to be on the safe side, ask whether your planned activity is covered. If it is not or if it is specifically excluded from the cover, find another insurer.

When things go wrong

If you buy wedding insurance, you have a measure of cover if your suppliers fail to deliver but only if it is because they have gone out of business. If they simply failed to deliver what you had ordered (and they are still in business) or failed to comply fully with the terms of your contract with them, insurance will not cover you because you can seek compensation directly from the supplier. The same is true if a wedding present you are given turns out to be faulty in some way.

The Sale of Goods Act 1979 (as amended) states that goods bought from a business must comply with their 'description' and 'be of satisfactory quality', so if you ask your florist to supply red roses, for example, you should not receive pink carnations; similarly, a spin dryer you are given as a wedding present should spin. The Supply of Goods and Services Act 1982 (common law in Scotland) states that 'services' supplied by a business should be carried out with 'reasonable care and skill'. For example: hired cars should not break down, marquees should not collapse and the photographs should not be blurred. If you book your honeymoon through a tour operator, you have added protection against a substandard holiday or against the tour operator going bust in the form of the Package Travel Regulations 1992.

If you feel that your suppliers have let you down and it is not possible to get the problem sorted out before the wedding, you can ask your supplier not only to refund your money but also to compensate you for any additional expenditure you may have incurred as a result of their incompetence. You may also be able to claim for the loss of enjoyment you suffered. Where contractors know that they are providing services for a wedding, the loss-of-enjoyment factor will be greater than usual because of the one-off nature of the event. If you have a complaint, you should make your dissatisfaction known clearly and politely to the person in charge and you should follow this up in writing, explaining what you want them to do to rectify the situation and the amount of financial compensation which you expect to receive. If your supplier ignores your complaint or fails to offer you satisfactory compensation, you can pursue the matter in the small claims court (sheriff court in Scotland).

Chapter 22

Financing your future

In purely financial terms, wedded bliss is well worthwhile: you may be able to pay less tax, your future pension will go up and, from the moment you sign your marriage certificate, you will automatically be entitled to at least some – if not all – of your spouse's wealth. How far your other finances are affected depends on more personal factors such as how joint you want your finances to be, how financially dependent one of you will be on the other and how keen you are to exploit the tax rules which favour the married state. (Remember to inform banks and financial institutions if you change your name.)

Some couples choose to draw up a prenuptial agreement, which covers how their assets would be divided in the event of a divorce. Although no one wants to consider divorce before they have even got married, some couples feel happier if they know where they stand financially. For more information on this, see pages 15–16.

Marriage and tax

Before April 1990, marriage meant that a man became responsible for his wife's tax affairs, and a woman's income from savings and investments was regarded as belonging to her husband, so he had to pay the tax on it. Since then, however, husband and wife are treated as individuals, with each responsible for their own tax affairs. This means that you will still get your own slice of tax-free income (your personal allowance), pay your own tax bill and, if applicable, have to fill in your own tax return. Apart from having to tell your tax office if you change your name, in practical terms you will see very little difference in your dealings with the Inland Revenue. Although married couples no longer get an extra personal allowance for having tied the knot, the tax system still looks favourably on married couples because:

- any **gifts** you make to each other will be free of tax
- you may be able to save tax by **rearranging the ownership of your savings and investments**.

Tax-free gifts

It may seem an odd concept that gifts attract tax at all but they do: in the form of inheritance tax for the recipient and capital gains tax for the person making certain sorts of gift (in general, things which can rise and fall in value such as antiques, property and shares). The tax rules for gifts largely exist to deter people from giving away their wealth before they die as a way of avoiding inheritance tax. So it is unlikely that you will have to tell your tax office about all your wedding presents – although it may be interested if they are very valuable. As soon as you are married, there is no need to worry about tax on anything you give to your spouse because gifts between husband and wife – whatever the gift is and whatever it is worth – are exempt from both inheritance tax and capital gains tax, which can work to your advantage (see below). The tax rules are also quite generous when it comes to wedding presents:

- before the wedding, the bride and groom can give each other gifts of up to £2,500
- each parent of the bride or groom can give one or other of them a gift up to the value of £5,000
- a grandparent (or great-grandparent) can give up to £2,500
- anyone else can give £1,000.

Note that if a gift exceeds the limits given above and the person making the gift dies within seven years of making it, there may be inheritance tax to pay if the donor's estate is worth more than a certain amount (£263,000 for deaths occurring in the 2004–5 tax year). If the gifts fall within the limits given above, there will be no inheritance tax to pay.

Your savings and investments

Because husbands and wives are taxed independently of each other, you will see no change in the way your savings and investments are

Tip

Strictly speaking, to qualify for their tax-free status, wedding gifts have to be made 'in consideration of the marriage' and 'conditionally on the marriage taking place', so encourage generous relatives to write you a letter which makes the reason for their gift clear.

taxed. However, you may want to rearrange your joint finances to make the most of the tax concessions available to married couples.

- If you have **savings or investments in joint names** – a joint building society account, for example – the income is automatically treated as being paid to you in equal shares, with each of you being responsible for paying the tax on your own share. However, if you own the savings or investments in unequal shares, you can ask your tax office to tax the income on that basis – so if you paid in a third of the money held in a joint savings account and your spouse paid in two thirds, you can ask to be taxed only on one third of the income.
- Perhaps more worthwhile – **if you and your spouse pay different rates of tax or one of you pays no tax at all** – is to put the savings and/or investments solely into the name of the spouse paying less or no tax. However, you have to be prepared to relinquish control over the money you give to your spouse so think carefully if you are not happy to do this.
- If you make a lot of **capital gains** – you dabble in the Stock Market, for example – and you regularly make full use of your own capital gains tax exemption of £8,200 (in the 2004–5 tax year) consider giving your spouse any investment that you would want to sell to make use of the fact that you each get your own £8,200 exemption. However, this will not help if your spouse also makes substantial capital gains and/or refuses to sell.

Marriage and your pension

Although it is probably not at the forefront of your mind as you plan for your big day, your pension may receive a substantial boost as soon as you have tied the knot – particularly if you are a woman.

If you belong to an employer's pension scheme, you are very likely to find that – without your having to increase your pension contributions – your spouse will automatically become entitled to receive a widow's or widower's pension and possibly a lump sum when you die. Depending on your spouse's National Insurance record, you may also qualify for a lump sum and allowance from the state.

If you have a personal pension, where your contributions build up a fund, this should be paid as a lump sum to your spouse in the event of your death. You can also arrange for your spouse to receive a pension if you die after retirement by buying what is called a 'joint life annuity' at the point that you decide to convert your pension pot into a pension income. The exception to this is where you have invested part of your National Insurance Contributions in a personal pension (these sorts of plans are variously called 'appropriate', 'rebate-only' or 'contracted-out' pension plans). These pension plans must make provision for a pension to be paid to your widow or widower (if 45 or over at the time of your death unless you have children).

Whichever sort of pension you have, make sure that the provider of it knows that you have married. You should tell the Inland Revenue★ (the government department now in charge of National Insurance Contributions) that you are now married as a matter of course.

Marriage, money and property: wills (England and Wales)

There is more to the toast 'health, wealth and happiness' than you may have imagined because (unless you live in Scotland, see page 212) as soon as you marry, your spouse automatically becomes entitled to at least £125,000 of all your worldly goods. This is because your marriage automatically declares any will you may have made as a single person null and void (in legal parlance, your marriage 'revokes' the earlier will). If you want to be confident that in the event of your death your spouse will inherit all that you own, you will have to make another will in his or her favour. If you do not do this, the law decides how much he or she will get and shares out your estate – everything you own after subtracting debts and any jointly owned assets, such as your home – as follows (note that the amount of the limits given below may change from time to time):

- if your estate is worth less than £200,000 (less than £125,000 if you have children) your spouse gets everything
- if your estate is worth more than £200,000, your spouse gets £200,000 plus half the remaining estate. The rest passes to whichever generation of relatives is still alive in this order: your parents, your siblings, your nephews and nieces. If there are no relatives to inherit the remainder of the estate, your spouse gets everything
- if your estate is worth more than £200,000 and you have children, your spouse gets £125,000 plus the right to the use of and/or income from (called a life interest) half the remaining estate. Your children get the rest.

As well as making sure that your wealth goes to those people you want to have it, making a will simplifies and shortens the process of sorting out your affairs. Making a new will after your marriage is particularly important if you have children from an earlier liaison and you want them to inherit part of your estate.

Making a new will is less urgent if your matrimonial home is your main asset and it is already in your joint names since half of it, if you are 'tenants in common', will pass to your spouse through the intestacy provisions; if you are 'joint tenants', the share will pass automatically to your spouse whether or not you make a will, i.e. by survivorship.

Tip

If you want to avoid the problem of being without a will from your wedding day until you have time to make a new one after your marriage, consult your legal adviser before your wedding. Your adviser should be able to draw up a specially worded will that will not be automatically revoked by your marriage. This should say that the will is made in contemplation of marriage to a named person and it should also specifically state that the person whose will it is (the testator) intends that the will shall not be revoked by his or her marriage to the named person.

Wills in Scotland

If your permanent home is in Scotland and you die without making a will, the rules are different from those in England, Wales and Northern Ireland. Your spouse gets the house or flat (up to £110,000 in value), furniture (up to a value of £20,000) and a cash sum of £50,000 provided that there are no children or other descendants. If there are, the cash sum is reduced to £30,000. Your spouse is also entitled to half (a third if there are children) the remaining 'movable' estate – which means anything that is not land or buildings. If there is anything left after that, the remainder goes to the nearest relatives of the person who died following this order: children, grandchildren, great-grandchildren, then siblings and finally parents.

Tip

To find out more about tax and marriage, ask your tax office for leaflet IR8o *Income tax and married couples.*

Marriage and your joint finances

Although you have little say in the way marriage affects your tax, pension or right to inherit, it is entirely up to you whether or not marriage has an effect on your day-to-day finances. However, it is worth spending time talking about how you will organise your finances, not least because it could spare you a few rows: according to a survey conducted early in 1998 for Relate* (the relationship-counselling charity), money came top of the list of the reasons for marital strife, with nearly half the people in the survey saying that it was the most common cause of arguments.

If you were living together before you married, you will probably have come to some arrangement for sharing the household bills and other joint spending. However, if you are setting up home together for the first time, it would be worthwhile deciding:

* what you both agree is joint spending
* what you are each going to contribute to joint spending

- what you both agree is personal (and private) spending
- who is going to pay for what
- how you are going to share bills
- how you are going to share your assets – your home or shares, for example
- who is going to be in charge of the finances
- how you will agree spending priorities
- how you will make financial plans for the future – whether it is saving for a holiday or for when you have children.

Once you have decided all that, you will be in a position to see if you need to make any adjustments to your existing financial arrangements, such as making your bank account a joint one or arranging for your spouse to be the joint owner of your home.

Warning

According to Relate*, lack of openness in financial arrangements can be a major source of friction and can even point to an underlying lack of trust in other areas of your relationship. In the Relate survey, women were found to be particularly sensitive to trust and secrecy issues related to money.

Joint and separate bank accounts

If you decide that you are going to pool your resources (whether in whole or in part) to pay for what you have decided is joint spending, you may find it useful to open a joint bank account. You can either run this alongside your own personal current accounts – because you want to keep some of your finances separate and private, for example – or you can arrange for both your salaries (if applicable) to be paid into a joint account and close your sole accounts. An alternative, if you want to share everything with your spouse but you do not want to close your sole account – because it is convenient for work, for example – is to make both your sole accounts joint ones.

You will have to open the joint account together, but whether you both have to sign cheques is up to you. Once the account is open, you will each get your own cheque book, cheque guarantee card (provided the bank is happy to provide this straight away), payment and cash card (or 'multi-function' card which combines all three types of card). You will also become joint owners of the money in the account and jointly responsible for any debts (called 'joint and several liability'). This means that your current account provider can recover money to pay off debts from either account holder regardless of who actually spent the money.

The same is true if you arrange for your spouse to be an additional cardholder on your credit card. However, if you each have an existing credit card in your pre-marriage names, there is no particularly good reason for changing the arrangement – especially since having two different cards gives you more flexibility and possibly a higher joint credit limit. The only situation in which it could be worth making your spouse an extra cardholder on your credit card is if he or she has been refused a credit card of his or her own.

Warning

If you have a very different attitude towards money from that of your partner – one of you is a saver while the other is a spendthrift, for example – you may find it less stressful to keep your financial arrangements separate.

Medical insurance

If you have private medical insurance (which aims to pay for private health care) either through your job or that you have bought yourself, make sure that your employer or the insurer knows that you have married. If you want your spouse to benefit from the policy, you may find that it does not cost that much more to cover him or her under a joint policy.

Life insurance

If you want your spouse to benefit from any life insurance you have, you will need to tell your employers (if they provide death-in-service benefits) and also your insurers that you have married. It would also be a good idea to check that the policies are 'written in trust' to your spouse so that the proceeds will be paid directly to him or her. This has two advantages: the money can be paid more quickly, and it does not count towards your estate for inheritance tax purposes.

Appendix: Wedding law

Anyone getting married in the UK must meet the legal require-ments, whether they are having a civil wedding or a religious wedding of any denomination.

The law in England and Wales

The basic rules that apply to all marriages in England and Wales are:

- the couple must be of different sexes
- you must be aged 16 or over but you need your parents' written consent if you are under the age of 18
- you must be free to marry, i.e. you must not be related to each other in any of the ways specified on pages 227–8. Also if either party has been married previously, the former marriage must have been ended by decree in the appropriate court
- you must have two witnesses
- the wedding must take place in a district register office, in any premises approved by the local authority for marriages (hotel, stately home etc.), in a church or chapel of the Church of England or Church in Wales, in a military chapel, a synagogue or in any other place of worship that has been registered by the General Register Office for England and Wales★ for the solem-nisation of marriages.

The White Paper, *Civil Registration: Vital Change*, published in January 2002, set out the government's plans for reform of marriage law. It explained that a celebrant-based system of marriage would be introduced, with no legal restrictions on the day, time or place of marriage. Celebrants would be either civil or religious, and either would be able to perform marriage ceremonies anywhere within England or Wales. This will allow couples more flexibility, and a greater choice of venues. A change in the law is necessary to implement these proposals, and this could happen in late 2005/early 2006.

The service may not be conducted privately – which means that the doors may not be locked during the ceremony, thereby preventing potential bona fide objectors being present. The marriage (both civil and religious) may take place on any day at any time between 8am and 6pm and need only be in front of two witnesses, who can be total strangers to each other and to you. (These restrictions do not apply to Jewish or Quaker weddings.)

The law in Scotland

Marriage law in Scotland differs in a few crucial ways. The minimum legal age is 16 whether you have parental consent or not.

There are no restrictions on the time or place at which a religious marriage can take place as long as the legal and civil requirements are met. In theory, you are free to marry outdoors at midnight if you can find an authorised minister to conduct the ceremony. Civil weddings in Scotland may now take place either in a register office, or at an approved place, by arrangement with the registrar. A list of approved places is available from the General Register Office for Scotland*. Scottish law permits couples to marry on board a boat, which does not have to be moored, although it must remain within the boundary of the registration district in which notice of marriage was given for the duration of the ceremony. Couples may also marry in their own homes. A licence would have to be issued first, and a registrar would have to perform the ceremony.

Documents required for marriage

For a civil wedding in the UK, when making a marriage application to the registrar you should take your full current passport. If this is not available you will need to produce two documents such as a cheque book or birth certificate. For a church wedding you will need to show your certificate of baptism to the minister (and confirmation certificate, in the case of the Roman Catholic Church). Most churches require at least one of you to be baptised. If you are marrying for the second time you will need to show your decree absolute or the death certificate of your former spouse. If you are under the age of 18 consent from your parents or guardians will normally be required.

Setting the date

In the case of both civil and religious weddings in England or Wales, the date of the marriage can be set up to a year in advance, and you may be able to make a provisional booking further ahead than this. In Scotland, the amount of advance notice needed is left to the discretion of the minister or registrar, provided it meets with Scottish legal requirements (see page 217), but couples are advised to make enquiries of the minister or registrar well in advance, particularly if they live in a town or city.

Civil weddings in England and Wales

As outlined on page 216, there are plans to change the law on marriage, including that which governs civil weddings. These changes could become law in late 2005/early 2006. Changes would be made to make giving notice easier for people who do not live and work in the same place, or who have difficulty getting to the register office during normal working hours. Under the proposed new laws, bride and groom would be able to visit different registration authorities to give notice of their intention to marry. Information contained in the notice would be kept on a central database.

Under the proposed new laws, instead of the venue being 'approved', it would be the civil celebrant who was authorised. This would mean that civil marriages could take place in any location, including the couple's home, or at an outdoor venue. For up-to-date information on these changes, visit the website of the General Register Office for England and Wales*.

At the time of writing (March 2004) the procedure for giving notice for a civil marriage in England and Wales is governed by changes made in 2001 to the Marriage Act 1949, as follows:

- Notice must be given **in person** by **both** parties to the marriage to the superintendent registrar at the register office in the district where you both live. If you live in the same district you should attend your local register office together to give notice. If you live in different districts then you must each give notice separately in your own district.
- Both of you must have lived in a registration district in England or Wales for at least seven days before giving notice of your intention to marry. You must give a minimum of 15 days' and a maximum of 12 months' notice of your intention to marry. After giving notice you must wait for a further 15 clear days before the marriage can take place. For example if you give notice on 1 June, you can marry on or after 17 June. If you make an advance booking more than one year ahead, it is essential that you also give formal notice as soon as you are legally able to do so.
- Each party to the marriage will be asked to declare his or her nationality.

When the superintendent registrar has accepted the notice, it is then entered into the marriage notice book and also displayed on a public notice board for 15 days. This provides the opportunity for anyone who has an objection to your proposed marriage to make a statement. After 15 days, you may apply for the certificate of authority for the marriage to proceed. This is not the same thing as a marriage certificate, which you can request after your wedding. If your notice of marriage is being displayed in two districts you must ensure both certificates of authority for the marriage are available prior to the wedding, as you will be asked to produce them before the ceremony can go ahead.

The fee for giving notice is £30 each (i.e. £60 per couple), and at a register office you will also have to pay a fee of £34 to the registrar for attending your marriage, plus £3.50 for a marriage certificate which is issued after the ceremony, making a total cost of £97.50. At approved premises, as well as the £60 fee for giving notice, you will also have to pay a fee for the superintendent registrar and a registrar to attend. These fees are set by the local authority, and vary across the country. A charge will also be made for the use of the premises.

The date of your marriage can be set to take place at any time within a year of when the notice was given. If you find that you wish to postpone the wedding beyond that time you will have to apply and pay for a notice (or notices) again.

If you are marrying at a register office which is not in the district(s) where you reside, you should discuss making a provisional booking with the superintendant registrar of that district to attend your marriage, which can be confirmed when the certificate(s) of authority are issued.

Remarriage in a civil setting

You will need to provide proof of how the previous marriage ended. This could be a divorce absolute document, with the original court seal, or a death certificate or a certified copy; photocopies of these documents are not acceptable.

After taking personal details, the registrar will ask you to sign a declaration that you are eligible to marry. A false declaration could invalidate the marriage and may render you liable to prosecution under the Perjury Act, with the further possible offence of bigamy being taken into account.

Church of England weddings

If you are getting married in an Anglican church the form of service must be agreed with the minister. There are three permitted options: the traditional *Book of Common Prayer* service, the slightly revised (1966) form of that service or *The 2000 Marriage Service* (Common Worship).

The system of reading marriage banns, and the requirement that people must live in the parish in which they marry, is currently under review, and a change in the law is expected in late 2005/early 2006. When this happens, a new system of joint church/state preliminaries will be introduced, the current usage of banns will be removed, and it will be the religious celebrant who is authorised, rather than the marriage venue. It is not yet clear exactly how the change in the law will affect couples planning a church wedding. For up-to-date information, visit the website of the Church of England★ or that of the General Register Office for England and Wales★.

At the time of writing (early 2004), the law remains as below:

Marriage by banns

You should agree the date of your wedding with the minister at the earliest opportunity. If either (or both) of you lives in the parish where you are to marry, the minister will arrange to have banns read in the church on three Sundays prior to the wedding. This is usually on consecutive Sundays and must be carried out within three months of the date of the wedding. It is customary for the couple to attend the service on those three Sundays to hear their banns read. The purpose of the banns is to make public your intention to marry and to invite any objections to the ceremony taking place. The fee for the calling of banns is £15. If one of you lives in another parish the banns must also be read in that church for which the same fee is charged, and in addition a banns certificate must be obtained from the minister of the second church, for which the fee is £9. In addition, you may choose to be married in the church where one (or both) of you worships and is on the church electoral role. In that event the banns must be called in that church and also in the parish or parishes where you both live. Banns are not called if the marriage takes place by common or special licence, as described below.

Marriage by common licence

This is used when the parties to the marriage are resident in a particular parish only temporarily, which must be a minimum of 15 consecutive days before the licence is issued. It is also used where one party to the marriage, who normally lives in England, does not have British nationality, or where one party is a British national who normally lives abroad.

As with banns, one of you must be living in the parish where you are to marry, or be on the church electoral roll, and the minister will be able to advise about applying for the licence. Where a licence has been obtained no banns are called, but an affidavit – verifying the details given and that there is nothing in law to prevent the marriage – has to be sworn. The affidavit must be sworn within the three-month period before the date of the wedding. You should note that common licences are not available if one of you has been divorced (and the former spouse is still living) and it is also a requirement that at least one of you must be baptised. The fee for a common licence is currently £55.

Marriage by special licence

This licence is issued on the authority of the Archbishop of Canterbury, and exceptional reasons must be given why one of the other preliminaries on page 221 cannot be used. It is generally used where neither of you is resident in the parish where you wish to marry or if the wedding is to take place in an unlicensed building, such as a private chapel. These licences are issued by the Faculty Office*, which you should approach after consultation with the minister. Again, special licences are not available where one party is divorced, with a former spouse still living, or where neither party is baptised. The fee is currently £125.

Remarriage and the Church of England

In 2002 the General Synod rescinded the marriage resolutions of the Canterbury and York Convocations, which had exhorted clergy not to marry anyone who had a former spouse still living. The Synod supported a motion which affirmed that, while marriage should always be taken as a solemn, public and lifelong covenant between a man and a woman, some marriages regrettably do fail and that there are exceptional circumstances in which a divorced person may be married in church during the lifetime of a former spouse.

This motion makes it clear that there is no guaranteed right for couples, of whom one or both parties is divorced, to remarry in church. It also acknowledges that some members of the clergy feel unable to conduct such marriages under any circumstances, as a matter of conscience. A minister's refusal is final, and there is no process of appeal to the Bishop. Nor is it currently possible, because of the legal restrictions on where couples may marry, for divorcees to seek another church where there may be a sympathetic minister who is prepared to take the service.

The Church has now produced guidelines for ministers, which they can use with couples who want to discuss the possibility of a religious ceremony, and a leaflet and application form are available for couples. More details are on the Church of England* website.

In some cases, a service of blessing can be given for married couples who wish to renew their vows, or for couples who have had a civil wedding but wish to add this religious ceremony. Not all clergy are happy to take a 'repeat' service – and some will not do so. However, as there is no residence requirement involved, couples are not restricted to their parish church. The blessing service usually consists of a version of the marriage service itself, but has no legal validity (e.g. no entry will be made in the marriage register). Make it clear beforehand if you hope to have hymns, bridesmaids, flowers and wear traditional wedding clothes to your service of blessing, as some ministers do not approve of this. See page 30 for more details.

Marriage in Scotland

For both civil and religious weddings in Scotland a minimum period of 15 days' notice must be given to the registrar in the district where the wedding is to be held, although four to six weeks' notice is preferred. Banns are no longer required for a religious ceremony. A schedule is then issued to the bride or groom up to seven days before the religious ceremony. It must be given to the minister before the service. For a civil wedding the schedule remains at the register office.

The order and content of the marriage service may be amended, and the minister or registrar may agree to the inclusion of non-scriptural readings of poems or prose. There is no residency requirement for marrying in Scotland, and there is no equivalent to the decree nisi, so you can remarry directly after the divorce is announced.

Marriage in Northern Ireland

The preliminaries to marriages have been completely changed by the Marriage (Northern Ireland) Order 2003 which came into effect on 1 January 2004. The main changes contained in the new legislation are:

- Notice for all marriages (including religious marriages) is given by **both parties** to the registrar in the district where the marriage is to take place, at least 14 days before the proposed date of marriage. Notice can be given by post, and there are no residency requirements, either in the district or in Northern Ireland. The registrar will issue a schedule, that allows the marriage to take place, to be given to the officiant. When the marriage ceremony is completed the schedule is signed by the officiant, the parties and two witnesses, before it is returned to the registrar for registration, after which the marriage certificates can be issued.

- Religious marriages will be conducted by authorised officiants (ministers, priests, pastors etc., in properly constituted religious bodies). There are now no registered buildings, and all authorised religious officiants may conduct marriages where the religious bodies consider appropriate.
- Civil marriages may be conducted by a registrar in 'Approved Places' such as hotels, stately homes, which have been authorised by district councils, and may take place at any time, and on any day including Sunday.

Roman Catholic weddings

Anyone having a Roman Catholic wedding must give notice to the superintendent registrar (see pages 218–19), and in some cases the registrar must be present at the religious ceremony, though often the minister will be the registrar himself.

A Roman Catholic priest may insist on a lengthy period (usually at least six months) of notice of your intention to marry, as it is regarded as essential for you to prepare properly for such a serious commitment. If the marriage is mixed (i.e. one of you is not Roman Catholic), the parish priest will have to apply for special permission on your behalf. Both ministers can attend the ceremony.

Remarriage and the Roman Catholic church

If either the bride or groom is divorced the couple are not permitted to have a Roman Catholic wedding; only those whose former partner is deceased or whose marriage was annulled (i.e. declared not to have been valid in the first place) can have a Roman Catholic ceremony.

Jewish weddings

A couple wishing to marry in a synagogue should give notice at a register office of their intention to marry (see pages 218–19). The certificate or certificates of authority for marriage are issued to the secretary of the synagogue, and the declaratory and contracting words required to make the marriage legal are incorporated within the religious ceremony. Alternatively, couples may have a separate civil wedding at a register office, and a purely religious ceremony in the synagogue at another time. Jewish weddings can take place anywhere – in a synagogue, private house, hired hall or in the open air – as long as they are held under the *chuppah* or wedding canopy, which symbolises home, and the couple has the necessary legal document (certificate of authority for marriage, see page 219). The ceremony can be celebrated at any time, except during the Jewish Sabbath (from sunset on Friday until sunset on Saturday) or on festival or fast days. It must also be performed in the presence of 10 men, and two witnesses who are not related to either the bride or groom. Both the latter must be of the Jewish faith and free to marry. If either the bride or the groom is not Jewish, he or she must convert before getting married. The process is long and demanding, involving instruction and an examination. The groom must be a member of the synagogue in which the couple is to marry.

Remarriage in the Jewish faith

If either the bride or groom or both is divorced they must produce the decree absolute and the Jewish bill of divorce.

Nonconformist or Free Church, Muslim, Hindu and Sikh weddings

Nonconformist or Free Churches such as the Methodists, United Reformed Church, Baptists and Presbyterians and the Orthodox Church all require you to go to your local register office and apply to the superintendent registrar for a certificate of authority for the marriage to proceed. The same applies to Muslim, Hindu and Sikh weddings. The certificate or certificates of authority for marriage should be given to the registrar or other person who is to register the marriage. The declaratory and contracting words required to make the marriage legal are incorporated within the religious ceremony. Whether you will need a registrar to attend the religious ceremony itself depends on whether there is a person in your place of worship licensed to act as a registrar (this may be the minister or the priest) to witness your marriage. In addition to the 'authorised person' the marriage must be witnessed by at least two people.

Quaker weddings

The Religious Society of Friends* (Quakers) has its own registering officers, who are allowed by law to witness the marriage and the signing of the marriage certificate. Those wishing to marry must go to their local register office and apply to the superintendent registrar for a certificate of authority for the marriage to proceed. They must also apply to the registering officer of the monthly meeting ('meeting' is the name given to the local Quaker community) of the area in which they intend to get married. Ideally, those in formal membership should do this at least three months before the planned date (and certainly no less than six weeks before). Those not in formal membership may marry, provided they are in sympathy with Quaker principles and practice and they are known to, and their application to marry is supported by, local Quakers. They should consult the registering officer or a local overseer (responsible for pastoral care) and allow extra time. The couple must then complete a declaration of intention of marriage. All the legal requirements for a wedding in England and Wales or in Scotland must also be met. Notice of the intention to marry is then made public at the meetings. Remarriage after divorce is a pastoral matter, at the discretion of the local Quaker meeting.

Marriage certificates

On the day of your wedding at a register office or approved premises, you can purchase a marriage certificate for £3.50. This is optional but a very useful document to have in your possession. You will both be asked to disclose your addresses at the time of your marriage and your ranks or professions. The certificate also includes your natural or adoptive fathers' names as well as their ranks or occupations. If for any reason either of you does not wish to reveal this information there is no legal obligation to do so.

Marrying abroad

Be sure to check all legal requirements for the wedding as they can differ from country to country. When looking through the brochure or making an initial enquiry check whether you need:

- a 10-year passport
- a visa
- your birth certificate
- return tickets to the UK
- proof of address
- your original decree absolute, if divorced; or former partner's death certificate, plus original marriage certificate
- parental consent if you are under 18 (21 in some countries)
- proof of vaccinations, if required
- if one of you is adopted, an adoption certificate
- deed poll for any name change
- certificate of baptism for church wedding
- certificate of confirmation for Catholic wedding.

If you require documents you should take originals, or copies certified by a notary, although some countries require you to send them in advance.

If your wedding is not being arranged through a travel agent check the minimum length of time you have to be resident as this can vary from two days to several months. Prior to leaving the UK find out from the consulate, embassy or High Commission of the country in which you wish to marry what the legal requirements are.

People you may not marry

It is forbidden in the United Kingdom for a man or a woman to marry certain blood relations. However, contrary to popular belief, first cousins are not prohibited from marrying. It is worth noting that some religions do not allow marriage between other relations.

Blood relatives

A man may not marry his: mother, sister, daughter, father's mother (paternal grandmother), mother's mother (maternal grand-mother), son's daughter (granddaughter), daughter's daughter (granddaughter), father's sister (aunt), mother's sister (aunt), brother's daughter (niece), sister's daughter (niece).

A woman may not marry her: father, brother, son, father's father (paternal grandfather), mother's father (maternal grandfather), son's son (grandson), daughter's son (grandson), father's brother (uncle), mother's brother (uncle), brother's son (nephew), sister's son (nephew). These restrictions apply to half-blood relations and persons born out of wedlock.

Adopted relatives

If the adoption was authorised by an order of the court under the Adoption Act then the above restrictions apply. These are not removed even if another person has by a subsequent order been authorised to adopt the same person.

Step-relatives

Step-relatives aged 21 or more may marry provided that the younger member of the couple has at no time, before the age of 18, lived under the same roof as the older person. Neither must he or she have been treated as a child of the older person's family. Unless these conditions are met a man may not marry a: daughter of a former wife, former wife of his father, former wife of his father's father, former wife of his mother's father, daughter of a son of a former wife, daughter of a daughter of a former wife.

A woman may not marry a: son of a former husband, former husband of her mother, former husband of her father's mother, former husband of her mother's mother, son of a son of a former husband, son of a daughter of a former husband.

Relatives you may marry

The law was relaxed in 1960 to allow a man to marry his former wife's sister, aunt or niece and the former wife of his brother, uncle or nephew. Under previous legislation, these unions were prohibited unless the former spouse was deceased. The revisions in the law also apply to women.

The former spouses (in either or both cases) must be deceased if a man intends to marry the mother of a former wife or the former wife of a son, or if a woman intends to marry the father of a former husband or the former husband of a daughter.

Contacts

Civil and religious preliminaries and ceremonies

Association of Interchurch Families
Interchurch House
35–41 Lower Marsh
London SE1 7RL
Tel: 020-7523 2152
Fax: 020-7928 0010
Email: aif@ctbi.org.uk
Website:
www.interchurchfamilies.org.uk

Baptist Union
Baptist House
PO Box 44
129 The Broadway
Didcot
Oxfordshire OX11 8RT
Tel: (01235) 517700
Fax: (01235) 517715
Email: info@baptist.org.uk
Website: www.baptist.org.uk

Catholic Enquiry Office
The Chase Centre
114 West Heath Road
London NW3 7TX
Tel: 020-8458 3316
Fax: 020-8905 5780
Email: ceo@cms.org.uk
Website: www.cms.org.uk

Church of England
General Synod of the Church of
England
Enquiry Centre
Church House
Great Smith Street
London SW1P 3NZ
Tel: 020-7898 1000
Fax: 020-7222 6672
Website: www.cofe.anglican.org
The Enquiry Centre provides information about marriages in the Churches of England and Wales. For a downloadable leaflet, Marriage in church after divorce, *and application form for couples seeking remarriage, visit:*
www.
cofe.anglican.org/papers/mcad.pdf
This leaflet, and other publications, are also available from:
Church House Bookshop
31 Great Smith Street
London SW1P 3BN
Tel: 020-7898 1300
Fax: 020-7898 1305
Website: www.chbookshop.co.uk

Church of Scotland
121 George Street
Edinburgh EH2 4YN
Tel: 0131-225 5722
Email: swilson@cofscotland.org.uk
Website:
www.churchofscotland.org.uk

Council of Christians and Jews
5th Floor, Camelford House
89 Albert Embankment
London SE1 7TP
Tel: 020-7820 0090
Fax: 020-7820 0504
Email: cjrelations@ccj.org.uk
Website: www.ccj.org.uk
Offers advice to Christian/Jewish couples

Faculty Office of the Archbishop of Canterbury
1 The Sanctuary
Westminster
London SW1P 3JT
Tel: 020-7222 5381
Fax: 020-7222 7502
Website: www.facultyoffice.org.uk

Federation of Synagogues
65 Watford Way
London NW4 3AQ
Tel: 020-8202 2263
Fax: 020-8203 0610
Email:
info@federationofsynagogues.com
Website:
www.federationofsynagogues.com

General Register Office for England and Wales
Marriages Section
Smedley Hydro
Trafalgar Road
Birkdale
Southport PR8 2HH
Tel: (0870) 243 7788
(Monday–Friday 8am–8pm,
Saturday 9am–4pm)
Fax: (01704) 550013
Email: marriages.gro@ons.gov.uk
Website: www.statistics.gov.uk/
registration/general_register.asp
Advice and information about civil marriages in England and Wales
List of approved premises is available to view online at:
www.statistics.gov.uk/registration/
premises/default.asp

Printed version also available for £5, from:
Local Services
PO Box 56
Southport PR8 2GL
Tel: 0151-471 4817
Email: local.services@ons.gov.uk

General Register Office for Scotland
Marriage Section
New Register House
3 West Register Street
Edinburgh EH1 3YT
Tel: 0131-314 4447
Fax: 0131-314 4532
Email: marriage@gro-scotland.gov.uk
Website: www.gro-scotland.gov.uk/
The website gives all the information you need to marry in Scotland, including downloadable documents and a list of all the register offices and approved places

General Register Office (Northern Ireland)
Oxford House
49–55 Chichester Street
Belfast BT1 4HL
Tel: 028-9025 2036/7
Fax: 028-9025 2136
Email: groreg.nisra@dfpni.gov.uk
Website: www.groni.gov.uk

Hindunet.org
Website: www.hindunet.org

The Islamic Shari'a Council
34 Francis Road
Leyton
London E10 6PW
Tel: 020-8558 0581
Fax: 020-8558 7872
Email: info@islamic-sharia.co.uk
Website: www.islamic-sharia.co.uk
Information on Muslim wedding law and procedure

Jewish Marriage Council
23 Ravenshurst Avenue
London NW4 4EE
Tel: 020-8203 6311
Fax: 020-8203 8727
Email: jmc@brijnet.org
Website: www.jmc-uk.org

London Beth Din (United Synagogue)
Adler House
735 High Road
London N12 0US
Tel: 020-8343 8989
Fax: 020-8343 6262
Email: info@unitedsynagogue.org.uk
Website:
www.unitedsynagogue.org.uk
*Co-ordinates most conversions to Judaism
carried out in the UK*

Methodist Church
Secretary for Pastoral Care and
Spirituality
Methodist Church House
25 Marylebone Road
London NW1 5JR
Tel: 020-7486 5502
Email:
enquiries@methodistchurch.org.uk
Website: www.methodist.org.uk

Reform Synagogues of Great Britain
The Sternberg Centre
80 East End Road
London N3 2SY
Tel: 020-8349 5640
Email: admin@reformjudaism.org.uk
Website: www.reformjudaism.org.uk
Information on intermarriage

Religious Society of Friends (Quakers)
Friends House
173–177 Euston Road
London NW1 2BJ
Tel: 020-7663 1000
Fax: 020-7663 1001
Website: www.quaker.org.uk
*To find your nearest Quaker meeting,
look in your local telephone book under
'Quaker', visit the website, or telephone
head office, above*

**Unitarian and Free Christian
Churches**
Essex Hall
1–6 Essex Street
London WC2R 3HY
Tel: 020-7240 2384
Fax: 020-7240 3089
Email: ga@unitarian.org.uk
Website: www.unitarian.org.uk

United Reformed Church
Church House
86 Tavistock Place
London WC1H 9RT
Tel: 020-7916 2020
Fax: 020-7916 2021
Email: urc@urc.org.uk
Website: www.urc.org.uk

Marriage preparation

Before You Say 'I Do', Elizabeth
Martyn and Relate (Vermilion, 2003)
*Book using checklists, questionnaires and
case histories to reveal the keys to successful
relationships, and help couples achieve a
happy and lasting marriage*

Association of Marriage Enrichment
Website: www.ame-uk.org.uk
*Marriage preparation workshops and
questionnaires*

**fpa (formerly Family Planning
Association)**
2–12 Pentonville Road
London N1 9FP
Tel: 020-7837 5432
Fax: 020-7837 3042
Helpline: (0845) 310 1334
*Available Monday–Friday 9am–6pm for
advice and information on all matters
relating to contraception, sexual health and
clinic details*

Marriage Care (formerly the Catholic Marriage Advisory Council)
Clitherow House
1 Blythe Mews
Blythe Road
London W14 0NW
Tel: 020-7371 1341
Fax: 020-7371 4921
Email: info@marriagecare.org.uk
Website: www.marriagecare.org.uk
Offers marriage preparation courses

Relate
Herbert Gray College
Little Church Street
Rugby
Warwickshire CV21 3AP
Tel: (01788) 573241
Helpline: (0845) 456 1310
Fax: (01788) 535007
Email: enquiries@relate.org.uk
Website: www.relate.org.uk
Marriage preparation courses offered at some centres. Contact headquarters, or your local branch (number in phone book), for details

Alternative ceremonies

Rites and Ceremonies: A Practical Guide to Alternative Weddings,
Kate Gordon (Constable, 1998)

British Humanist Association
1 Gower Street
London WC1E 6HD
Tel: 020-7079 3580
Fax: 020-7079 3588
Email: info@humanism.org.uk
Website: www.humanism.org.uk
Publishes a book, Sharing the Future, *on organising a humanist wedding. Has details of local officiants*

Greater London Authority
City Hall
The Queen's Walk
London SE1 2AA
Tel: 020-7983 4000
Minicom: 020-7983 4458
Fax: 020-7983 4057
Email: mayor@london.gov.uk
Website: www.london.gov.uk

Lesbian and Gay Christian Movement
Oxford House
Derbyshire Street
London E2 6HG
Tel/Fax: 020-7339 1249
Email: lgcm@lgcm.org.uk
Website: www.lgcm.org.uk
Website gives details of how to apply for the names of ministers/priests who are willing to conduct a service of blessing

Pink Triangle Trust
34 Spring Lane
Kenilworth
Warwickshire CV8 2HB
Tel/Fax: (01926) 858450
Email:secretary@pinktriangle.org.uk
Website: www.pinktriangle.org.uk
Can arrange secular affirmation ceremonies of love and commitment for same-sex couples

Pink Weddings
Pad 108
15 Church Street
Weybridge
Surrey KT13 8AN
Tel: (01932) 571286
Fax: (0870) 130 2152
Email:
boyzngirlz@pinkweddings.biz
Website: www.pinkweddings.biz
Organises weddings and ceremonies for same-sex couples

Wedding legalities

Desktop Lawyer
Website: www.desktoplawyer.co.uk
*Online legal service. Prenuptial agreement
can be downloaded for £29.99*

DVLA
Customer Enquiries (Drivers) Unit
DVLC
Swansea SA6 7JL
Tel: (0870) 240 0009
Minicom: (01792) 782787
Fax: (01792) 783071
Email: drivers.dvla@gtnet.gov.uk
Website: www.dvla.gov.uk/

Inland Revenue
Website: www.inlandrevenue.gov.uk
Check phone book for your local office

Premium Bonds Office
National Savings and Investments
Blackpool
Lancashire FY3 9YP
Tel: (0845) 964 5000
Minicom: 0800 056 0585
Email:
customerenquiries@nsandi.com
Website: www.nationalsavings.co.uk

UK Deed Poll Service
PO Box 6788
Hatfield Peverel CM3 2WJ
Helpline: (0870) 350 1400
Fax: (0870) 350 1600
Email: enquiries@ukdps.co.uk
Website: www.deedpollsonline.com
*Advice and information on how to change
your name. You can make the change
online*

The United Kingdom Passport Service
Passport advice helpline:
(0870) 521 0410
Website: www.ukpa.gov.uk
*You can apply for a new passport, or
renew, amend or replace an existing one
by using downloadable application forms.
Forms are also available from Passport
Service High Street Partners, where you
can also get help with completing the
forms. Passports can also be issued by post
or in person through your district passport
office. Full details from the helpline or
website*

Wedding websites

Type 'weddings' into a search engine
such as www.google.co.uk, and you
will come up with thousands of sites.
For more information about services
available on the Internet, see page 66.

General information sites
www.confetti.co.uk

www.hitched.co.uk

www.weddingguideuk.com

www.webwedding.co.uk

www.bridesuk.net
*Website of Brides magazine, with useful
contacts for all sorts of wedding suppliers
nationwide*

www.weduk.com
*Directory site for wedding services in the
UK and Ireland. For links to wedding
insurers visit www.weduk.com/wedding-
insurance*

Advice and information for second marriages

www.confetti.co.uk
'Aunt Betti' can answer questions, and there is a chatroom where you can contact other couples

www.familyonwards.com
Website of author Jill Curtis, who will reply to queries. Site has detailed information about second marriages

Wedding venues

Many general wedding websites, such as *www.confetti.com* and *www.hitched.co.uk*, carry lists of venues for civil weddings

www.alternative-weddings.com
A paid-for service. You can order a specially compiled book of venues, buy a CD-ROM of all the venues listed on the database, or pay for one of 13 e-books of venues

www.perfectvenue.com
Interactive search site, with pictures and details of venues

www.theweddingdirectory.co.uk
Magazine published twice yearly and available from W H Smith, or view online at the website. Pictures and details of venues, plus other wedding services and suppliers

www.weddingvenues.co.uk
Website and quarterly magazine, available from newsagents, with details of venues by location

Wedding organisers

Check the general wedding websites, listed on page 233, or ask for recommendations from other couples in the confetti.com chatroom

www.alternative-occasions.co.uk
Can offer as much or as little co-ordination as couples choose

www.net-weddings.co.uk
Wedding co-ordinators, searchable by area

www.milestoneweddings.co.uk
Works on a fixed fee, but offers free personal consultation to start with

Wedding clothes

The general wedding websites (page 233) all have sections on clothes and good links

www.mossbros.com
Wedding clothes to hire for men. Wide range, including traditional morning dress. Branches nationwide

www.dejavubridalwear.co.uk
www.designer-bridalwear.co.uk
www.dreamdresses.co.uk
Sites where you can buy and sell once-worn bridal wear

Designer directory
*Website: www.macculloch.com
Lists bridal wear designers and dressmakers by area with contact details and approximate cost*

Dressmakers and dress patterns
www.sewbridal.co.uk
Internet source for McCall, Butterick and Vogue patterns

Butterick
For a list of dressmakers in your area, send £1 cheque made payable to Butterick Co Ltd to: Professional Dressmakers List, Butterick Co Ltd, New Lane, Havant, Hants PO9 2ND

Marriages abroad: tour operators

Kuoni Weddings
Tel: (01306) 747007
Email: help@kuoni.co.uk
Website:
www.kuoni.co.uk/weddings/

Thomas Cook
Tel: 0870 010 0437
Website: www.thomascook.com
For a customised electronic brochure to be emailed to you, visit:
www.thomascookpromotions.com/
brochures/default_tc.asp
General enquiries, email:
talktous@thomascook.com

Thomson Weddings in Paradise
Tel: (0870) 608 0169
Website: www.thomson.co.uk

Virgin Weddings
Tel: (0870) 990 8825
Website:
www.virginholidays.co.uk/weddings/
Weddings in USA, Caribbean and worldwide, including weddings at sea, at the Niagara Falls, in Disneyland or with an Elvis theme, as well as in more conventional settings

Photographs and videos

Association of Professional Videomakers
Ambler House
Helpringham
Lincolnshire NG34 0RB
Tel: (01529) 421717
Fax: (01529) 421742
Email: jan@videomakers.com
Website: www.apv.org.uk
Searchable database of wedding videomakers

Guild of Wedding Photographers UK
59 Fore Street
Trowbridge
Wiltshire BA14 8ET
Tel: (01225) 760088
Fax: (01225) 759159
Email: info@gwp-uk.co.uk
Website: www.gwp-uk.co.uk
Guild-qualified photographers, listed by area

Master Photographers Association Ltd
Jubilee House
1a Chancery Lane
Darlington
Co Durham DL1 5QP
Tel: (01325) 356555
Fax: (01325) 357813
Email: mpa@mpauk.com
Website: www.thempa.com
Searchable database of photographers

Society of Wedding and Portrait Photographers
Colomendy House
6 Bath Street
Rhyl LL18 3EB
Tel: (01745) 356935/356953
Email: info@swpp.co.uk
Website: www.swpp.co.uk
Searchable database of photographers

Wedding receptions and parties

Guild of International Toastmasters
Tel: 020-8852 4621
Website: www.guild-of-toastmasters.co.uk

Flowers and Plants Association
Tel: 020-7738 8044
Email: info@flowers.org.uk
Website: www.flowers.org.uk
Suggestions for flowers organised by colour, season and scent

Pressed for Time (UK) Ltd
37 Lower Swanwick Road
Southampton
Hampshire SO31 7HG
Tel: (01489) 574668
Email: info@pftuk.co.uk
Website: www.pftuk.co.uk
Will collect wedding bouquet from anywhere in the UK, photograph it, take it apart and create a picture of the bouquet using the petals and foliage

Music
Tel: 020-8314 1273
Email: info@cdsforlife.co.uk
Website: www.cdsforlife.co.uk
CDs of music suitable for civil and church weddings

Wedding Crèche Service Ltd
1 Netley Mill
Shere
Surrey GU5 9JT
Tel/Fax: (01483) 202490
Email: info@weddingcreche.com
Website: www.weddingcreche.com
Uses qualified staff to provide childcare and entertainment. Teams available in London, Bristol, Home Counties

Buying drink abroad
www.day-tripper.net

www.channelhoppers.net
Advice and information websites

www.sainsburys.co.uk/calais
Website of Calais branch; lets you order online

Wedding software

Wedding Magic wedding planner
Website:
www.frogwaresoftware.com

Wedding planner software
Wedding Package Stationery CD
Artworks
3 Pond Side
Wootton
Ulceby
North Lincolnshire DN39 6SF
Tel: (01469) 588138
Email: info@artsworksuk.com
Website: www.artworksuk.com
Stationery design package, costing £19.95, for producing wide range of co-ordinated wedding stationery

www.weddingwishes.co.uk
How to create your own wedding website

www.weddingclipart.com

www.ourspecialmoment.co.uk
Wedding website software

Wedding gifts

The general information sites (see page 233) have lots of suggestions and links related to gifts

www.ukshops.co.uk
Links to suppliers of a range of gifts

Online gift registries
www.blissonline.com
Online gift service

www.thegiftregistry.info

Same-sex partnerships

For up-to-date information on the Civil Partnership Bill

www.parliament.uk
www.stonewall.org.uk

Index

Baby Products

All parents want to give their baby the best start in life.
Newborn babies do not come with instructions, yet parents
have to make decisions about their child's comfort and safety
at what can be a vulnerable and emotional time. And
providing for a child can be a confusing and expensive
business.

Faced with the bewildering range of products available,
common-sense guidance – about what you *really* need – is
essential. *Baby Products* recommends safe and reliable options
across the price spectrum, helping you weigh up
manufacturers' claims objectively and make the right choice
for your baby. Incorporating findings of *Which?* reports, *Baby
Products* includes the latest advice in crucial areas such as child
car seats, shop-bought baby food and cot-death deterrence.
Equipment reviewed includes breast- and bottle-feeding
accessories; cots, cribs and bedding; nappies and changing
units; travel necessities; pushchairs, prams and buggies; baby
monitors and safety devices; toys; and toilet-training aids.

The book suggests where to shop, including mail order and
the Internet. Other parents share their experiences in helpful
hints and tips throughout.

Paperback   216 x 135mm   256 pages   £11.99

Available from bookshops, and by post from
Which?, Dept BKLIST, Castlemead,
Gascoyne Way, Hertford X, SG14 1LH
or phone FREE on (0800) 252100
quoting Dept BKLIST and your credit-card details

The Which? Guide to Good Hotels

Want to find a special place to stay? One that caters to *your* needs, rather than those of the owners? Consult *The Which? Guide to Good Hotels* for the cream of the crop. Crammed with descriptive detail, this guide selects hundreds of the best hotels, guesthouses and B&Bs throughout Britain to help you pick your ideal match – regardless of whether you are planning a romantic weekend, business trip or family holiday. The exciting candidates range from outposts of urban chic and chain hotels to country mansions, rural cottages and gastropubs.

All entrants are guaranteed to offer exceptional hospitality, outstanding cleanliness and friendly service. They are rated for quality, standards and comfort after a demanding inspection process, and our experienced team takes readers' reports into account to give a balanced assessment of each hotel.

The *Guide* refuses to accept payment for inclusion and remains firmly independent. Fully rewritten every year, its lively commentary will help you pick your star performers. The book includes:

- practical information about prices, facilities, opening times and directions
- symbols for hotels offering fine food, budget prices, a peaceful location and child-friendly facilities
- bargain rooms for under £35 per person per night
- colour photographs of award-winning hotels
- easy-to-read colour maps
- money-saving vouchers.

Paperback   232 x 144mm   544 pages   £15.99

Available from bookshops, and by post from
Which?, Dept BKLIST, Castlemead,
Gascoyne Way, Hertford X, SG14 1LH
or phone FREE on (0800) 252100
quoting Dept BKLIST and your credit-card details

The Good
Bed and Breakfast Guide

Britain's most widely respected and independent B&B guide presents over 900 establishments, as recommended by readers and backed up by inspectors. All have been handpicked for their friendly welcome, the thoughtful extras owners provide for their guests – for example, bathrobes and bike storage, breakfasts featuring home-made items – as well as perhaps a memorable setting or interesting history or architecture. The scope of accommodation is wide, from a white-washed thatched cottage in a sleepy hamlet, to an old manor house set in 300 acres of grounds, to a small townhouse perfectly placed for a short city break.

A description of the property precedes useful information on the number and types of rooms, prices, facilities such as a garden, sitting room and wheelchair access, and policy on children, one-night bookings and dogs.

Each new edition of *The Good Bed and Breakfast Guide*:

- is fully re-researched from the tip of Scotland to Land's End
- continues to focus on warmth of welcome, comfort and good value, with many rooms costing less than £25 per person per night
- includes full-colour maps and helpful lists
- features selected colour photographs of the Editor's Top 20 best B&Bs
- is totally independent and accepts no free hospitality, payment for inclusion or advertising.

Paperback   232 x 144mm   452 pages   £15.99

Available from bookshops, and by post from
Which?, Dept BKLIST, Castlemead,
Gascoyne Way, Hertford X, SG14 1LH
or phone FREE on (0800) 252100
quoting Dept BKLIST and your credit-card details